No More Mr. Nice Guy!

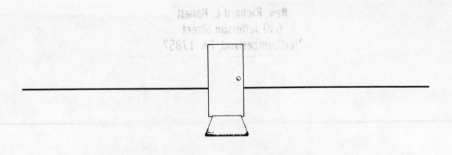

"This is a solid, no-nonsense, practical, and helpful book from one of America's outstanding Bible expositors, an extraordinarily gifted teacher. I very much enjoyed reading it."

Charles Colson
President
Prison Fellowship

"Steve Brown has a unique gift in cutting to the heart of matters that beset us. . . . His book is fresh; it is candid; it is alive. I loved reading every page of it."

R. C. Sproul
President
Ligonier Ministries

"With a delightful touch of impishness, Steve Brown tackles the subject of wimpishness. He is robust, readable, and right in what he says. I recommend this book to all who are wishing to be told that meekness is not weakness and that holy boldness is not only nice but necessary."

Stuart Briscoe
Pastor and Author

"This is the first of Steve Brown's books I have had the pure joy of seeing before the rest of the world. As I read it I felt like one of the chosen. Stephen Brown is a man whose wide study condenses in his mind and changes into powerful lasers of truth that rankle, challenge, and indict. . . .

"We have not met. Yet he stirs me to believe so, for his eyes have seen my friends, my world, my circumstances. His heart conceives my needs. . . . He helps me find ideals I had lost and brushes the dust from the old footprints of the Carpenter I once promised I would follow."

Calvin Miller
Pastor and Author of
The Singer Trilogy

"For Christians who feel like a zero with the naught rubbed out, here's a book that helps them to count. It teaches hard lessons in an easy style."

Haddon Robinson
President
Denver Conservative Baptist Seminary

"Steve Brown is a bold pastor who resents wimpishness in Christians. His book No More Mr. Nice Guy challenges his fellow Christians to leave the wimp stereotype and become the victorious models God intended and blesses."

Fred Smith
Author and Speaker

"I thank God for Steve Brown and his message in this book. In it he tells us how we can be bold as Christians while maintaining our individual personalities and traits, not conforming to a 'Christian mold' but being the individuals God created us to be. He also lets us know that even with Christ in us, we must realize that we're still human, that we still make mistakes, but that Christ's blood covers those mistakes, too."

Glenn Blackwood
Defensive Back
Miami Dolphins

"I have spent most of my life around coaches and athletes who don't mince any words when it comes to 'telling it like it is.' Thank God, Steve Brown tells it like it is in his new book, No More Mr. Nice Guy. Having played in the NFL for 14 years, I am still often asked, 'What was a nice guy like you doing in a place like that?' I see many parallels between my athletic career and my Christian life. Steve addresses and answers many of the questions I have asked about my faith—and challenges me in new areas of growth and maturity. The book is great!"

Norm Evans
President
Pro Athletes Outreach

"Few combine lively prose, clear logic, and abundant illustrations with the deftness and verve of Steve Brown. A biblical, compelling call to clear thinking and Christian integrity."

Harold L. Myra
President
Christianity Today, Inc.

Stephen Brown

No More Mr. Nice Guy!

GOODBYE

publishers since 1798

THOMAS NELSON PUBLISHERS
Nashville • Camden • New York

Published in Nashville, Tennessee, by Thomas Nelson, Inc. and distributed in Canada by Law-
son Falle, Ltd., Cambridge, Ontario.

Printed in the United States of America.

Scripture quotations are from THE NEW KING JAMES VERSION. Copyright © 1979, 1980,
1982, Thomas Nelson, Inc., Publishers.

Names, dates, and other details have been changed in the sample illustrations enclosed herein
to protect the confidentiality of pastoral counseling relationships.

Library of Congress Cataloging-in-publication Data

Brown, Stephen W.
  No more mr. nice guy!

  1. Christian life—Presbyterian authors. I. Title.
BV4501.2.B767   1986   248.4   86–8587
ISBN 0-8407-3139-6 PB

  3 4 5 6 7 8 9 10 - 97 96 95 94 93 92 91 90

In loving memory
of my brother, Ron,
who "got home
before the dark"
(Isa. 57:1–2)

Other Books by Stephen Brown

If God Is in Charge

Heirs with the Prince

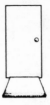

Contents

Acknowledgments

One of the problems with an acknowledgments page in a book is the danger of mentioning a few people who helped to the exclusion of many others who helped.

Given that so many people have helped me with this book . . .

given that I have probably absorbed a lot more information for this book from friends than I like to admit . . .

and given that when you see someone like me doing something like this you know he didn't do it by himself,

I hesitate to mention any names . . .

So I won't.

Foreword

I was shocked. My ears and eyes had to be playing tricks on me. I had just witnessed and heard a television talk-show host pose the following question to Dr. Martin Luther King: "Dr. King, is it true that black people are lazy, oversexed, and got rhythm?"

I could not believe that any white television host could be so blatantly insensitive as to ask a question like that of Martin Luther King. Yet as shocked as I was by the question, I was even more startled by King's answer. He replied, "Yes, it's true." Now my attention was riveted to the screen.

Dr. King explained his answer. He said, "If you tell people for two hundred years that they are lazy, oversexed, and got rhythm, sooner or later you will produce a generation of them that meet these standards."

At this point Dr. King was speaking wisdom. He was aware that people have a strong tendency to act out the role you create for them. We tend to do what society expects us to do. That is why it is crucial for groups and individuals to be alert to such imposed expectations.

For Christians in recent years, this tendency has had devastating consequences, because Western society has been telling us that we're supposed to be weak, insipid, and concerned only with what goes on inside the four walls of our church buildings. In a word, we're told we're supposed to be wimps, and many Christians have believed the lie.

If that weren't bad enough, there are also many Christians who believe *God* wants them to be wimps. They have misunderstood biblical teaching in the areas of love, submission, and turning the other cheek to one's enemies.

The result of this confusion is that while on the one hand a majority of Americans profess belief in God and Jesus Christ, and tens of millions claim to have been born again, on the other hand the influence of the church on the surrounding society has never been weaker. We Christians have lost our influence because we have bought the stereotype that we're to be seen but not heard, that our faith has nothing to say to the issues of the day and has no place in such crucial areas of life as government, law, education, science, and the arts.

On an individual level, Christians have bought the lie that it's better to be nice and to "get along" than it is to be right and stand up for the truth. We've accepted the notion that it's wrong to be different, both inside and outside the church. And we've allowed ourselves to be manipulated by guilt to the point that we're afraid to say no to anyone in the church, no matter what other responsibilities or priorities we already have.

What Steve Brown shows us in this excellent book is that God never intended for us to be wimps. Rather, he wants to free us from guilt and timidity to become the boldest, most dynamic and alive people in the world. As Paul wrote to his disciple Timothy, "God has not given us a spirit of fear, but of power and of love and of a sound mind" (2 Tim. 1:7). And Steve tells us *how* we can break out of the stereotypes that have bound us to become the kind of people our Father means for us to be.

When I became a Christian, I understood that Jesus took my sin away. What I have never heard from Him was that He intended to take my backbone away. The Christ I know does not destroy boldness, bravery, and challenging purpose; He enhances them. The Christ I know is a Christ who calls people to courage and to strength. We are to imitate Him. Whatever else Jesus was, He was a man. Nay, He was The Man.

One of my childhood heroes was Stan Musial. Though I lived in

Pittsburgh and Musial played for the St. Louis Cardinals, I still idolized him. He was, after all, from Donora, a steel town just south of Pittsburgh. I remember he had several nicknames including "Musicbox," "The Donora Dandy," and "The Rocking Chair Hitter" (because of his peculiar stance in the batter's box). But his most famous nickname was simply "The Man." He was, and still is, known as "Stan the Man."

In spite of my love and admiration for Stan Musial, however, I must demure at his ultimate nickname. Stan Musial is not "The Man." That sobriquet applies to one Man and to one Man only. That title belongs to Jesus. It was bestowed upon Him not by intention but by irony when Pontius Pilate displayed Christ before the howling mob. Hear Pilate announce before a hostile crowd, "*Ecce Homo*—Behold, The Man!"

That is what this book is ultimately about. Steve Brown has a unique gift in cutting to the heart of matters that beset us. Steve is a man's man. He has never surrendered to the call of wimpiness. He knows the Christ who stood before Pilate. His book is fresh; it is candid; it is alive. I loved reading every page of it.

R. C. Sproul
Orlando, Florida
Easter 1986

Introduction

Something has happened to the Christianity we have professed, something that smells like smoke and comes from the pit of hell. We have equated the word "Christianity" with the word "proper," "commitment" with "compromise," "love" with "sweetness," "servanthood" with "insipidity," and "sensitivity" with "banality."

It is possible, I suppose, that we are simply proper, compromising, sweet, insipid, banal people, and we adjust the Christian faith to conform to our emotional need to be that way. It could be that we have taken the eternal verities of the Bible and made them conform to American cultural standards so we can feel comfortable. But I don't believe that is the case with most Christians. I believe that many of us have "bought into" a Christianity that is neurotic and weak because we thought it was true Christianity. In other words, we have accepted someone else's neurosis as health.

In a recent Gallup survey, it was found that 79 percent of the general public in the United States claim to have made a personal commitment to Jesus Christ. When I read that statistic, I was absolutely amazed. If it is true, or even if it is only one-third true, there are enough Christians in the United States to revolutionize the world. But the last time I noticed, the world had not been revolutionized by Christians. The fact is that most of the Christians are in God's Secret Service. That's bad enough in itself. The real problem, however, is that somehow we have gotten the idea that it is Christian to be in God's Secret Service.

Three or four years ago I was involved in a gathering of Christians in Washington, D.C. It was an exciting time as some five hundred thousand Christians from across America gathered to make a positive witness for Christ in the nation's capital. At a luncheon preceding the main gathering, some of the leaders had an understandable anxiety about what was going to be happening during the mass demonstration. There were all sorts of questions racing through our minds: "What if the demonstration becomes, contrary to our plans, a partisan political demonstration?" "What if, in the enthusiasm of the moment, there is violence?" "How do you keep so many Christians, some of whom are very angry, from expressions of that anger?" "What if the press misinterprets what is going on?"

There was a formal program for the luncheon, but almost all of us were open to anything that would alleviate our anxiety. During a lull in the program, a black bishop rose from his chair and asked for the attention of the group. He said, "Brothers and sisters, I have a message from the Lord." The room became silent as the bishop continued. "The Lord says that if you Christians ever get over your fear, you are going to be dangerous."

This is a book about Christians' getting over their fear and becoming dangerous. It is a book about biblical boldness and the implications of biblical boldness as a way of life for the Christian. It is an effort to get back to the biblical truth of the Christian faith without the overtones of culture, tradition, and emotional needs. It is an effort to set the reader free from the wimp syndrome.

One of the interesting phenomena of our time is the increasing call for Christians to be involved in the public sector. For years evangelicals have made a hard division between sacred and secular with the general understanding that those two should never meet. Christians have been told that there was something "dirty" about politics, economics, and the arts. Now all that has changed, and I'm glad.

But it is hard to get over the habits of a lifetime; it is hard to feel free to do something that one has come to see as wrong and inappropriate for Christians. It is hard to live in the sunshine when one has spent most of one's life in a prison. That is what this book is all about. I don't want to tell you what to believe about politics, but I do want you to feel free to express what you believe. I don't want to tell you how or how much you should be involved in public education, but I do want you to feel free to be involved. I don't want to tell you what to read, see, and think, but I do want you to feel free to read, see, and think, and I certainly don't want others to tell you what you can read, see, and think. In other words, I want you to be free of man's restraints. I want you to be free to be what God wants you to be.

I will be saying some things in this book that may offend you. There will be times when you may feel that I have "gone too far" or have "said too much." You will perhaps think that I have been improper. If you feel that, please be patient. The Father is making me free, and when He does that it is hard to go back to the prison. Sunshine can be heady stuff. It could be that there will come a day when I will have to apologize for this book, but, again, maybe there will come a day when you will thank me for it.

Paul, in discussing the difference between law and grace, pointed to the difference between Hagar (the slave) and Sarah (the free). He said that Christians are not children of bondage. "Nevertheless what does the Scripture say? 'Cast out the bondwoman and her son, for the son of the bondwoman shall not be heir with the son of the free-woman.' So then, brethren, we are not children of the bondwoman but of the free. Stand fast therefore in the liberty by which Christ has made us free, and do not be entangled again with the yoke of bond-age" (Gal. 4:30–5:1). Jesus said that if we obeyed Him, He would tell us the truth and the truth would make us free. And then, as if to put an explanation on His teaching, He said, "Therefore if the Son makes you free, you shall be free indeed" (John 8:36).

It is my prayer that this book will help you to be free—really free. I want people to call you names. I just don't want them ever to call you a wimp.

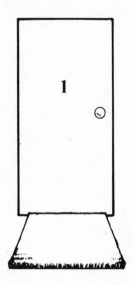

"Now when they saw the boldness of Peter and John, and perceived that they were uneducated and untrained men, they marveled."

ACTS 4:13

Stereotypes of a Saint

1

In David Mains's book *The Rise of the Religion of Antichristism*, Donald Wildmon, executive director of the National Federation for Decency, is quoted as saying, "In seven years of monitoring television, I have not seen one program, cast in a modern day setting, in which one person depicted as a Christian was shown as a warm, compassionate, intelligent person." Mr. Mains goes on to add his commentary:

> I'm not opposed to drama or humor or art or literature or the real-life situations that these forms so adequately present. But when Christians are regularly shown as wimpy, lackluster, two-faced, and mindless, with none of the courage or beauty or goodness or intellect that we know the church represents, I say there is a bias that needs to be called to account. And the accusing term to use is "antichristism."[1]

When you think about it, it makes you angry. But if you think you are angry, you ought to be a pastor. A friend of mine who has been married to a pastor for a number of years met a former classmate of hers at a class reunion. During the course of conversation my friend mentioned that she had married a pastor. A look of horror crossed the other woman's face, and in a voice dripping with sympathy she said, "Oh, I'm so sorry—sex is so wonderful." That says something disturbing about the pastoral stereotype.

It is interesting to watch the change that comes over people when they discover they have unknowingly been sitting next to, playing golf with, or talking to a pastor. There is always the pained expression, followed by the sheepish grin and then the half-hearted apology, "Reverend, why didn't you tell me? I can't believe all this time I didn't know. I sure hope I didn't say a curse word or something bad." I want to say, but only on occasion say it, "It's okay. My wife doesn't know either, or she would leave me."

Many Christians really think a pastor has a personal "hotline" to God and can rear back and perform a miracle almost any time he's inclined to do so. There are those in the church who believe that the pastor, if he isn't God, is a reasonable facsimile of same. And then there are, of course, those Christians who believe that pastors are a low form of life and they join the church to "get 'em." The pagans have a different image. They believe that a pastor is a sexless, anemic half-saint who would be out of place at anything other than a ladies-aid social, dressed in anything other than a black suit. There are times when I fully expect to walk into an airport somewhere and find three different bathrooms: "Ladies," "Men," and "Clergy." We all, including pastors, have trouble with the Christian stereotype.

WHAT THE WORLD THINKS OF US

Have you ever noticed how "objective" historians have conveniently deleted any reference to the Christian motivation of men and women in our past when that reference didn't fit their stereotype? Columbus, for instance, is seen as a courageous explorer with no mention of the fact that he was an explorer because he wanted to further the gospel of Christ and hasten the date of the second coming. We know about Washington's false teeth, but no history book includes his prayers or his commitment to Christ. Hardly anyone, except in passing, mentions the evangelical roots of almost every social reform in America. Wilberforce is a name most secular students of history never hear, and if they do, they don't know his deep commitment to Christ and the Christian roots of abolition that eventually swept from Wilberforce's England to America. Conversely, while Jonathan Edwards is perhaps the finest philosophical mind America ever produced, he is remembered only for his sermon "Sinners in the Hands of an Angry God" (a very good sermon, by the way). His presidency of Princeton and his great philosophical works are ignored. (Edwards's *The Freedom of the Will*, published in 1754, is a superior sampling of his philosophical writings.)

A number of young, single women in the church I serve have a constant problem with the passes they get from young pagan males. They tell me it is difficult to convince a pagan that they simply aren't interested. I suggested to a number of them that they give the man making the pass a mini-testimony of their relationship to Christ. Subsequent to my suggestion, a number of them came back to me and said, "It worked like magic. I waved the wand of Christ over his head and he disappeared!"

While that is an effective way to deal with the unwanted passes of pagans, I am disturbed when I think of why it may be so effective. It could be that no red-blooded American boy wants to be associated with a Christian woman because he has a stereotypic image of her that is somewhat less than flattering.

In a very critical review (one with which, incidentally, I disagree) by Aram Bakshian, Jr., of the "Mr. Rogers' Neighborhood" program, Mr. Bakshian writes:

Mr. Rogers is the perfect neutral babysitter. A kindly, chinless person with grey hair, grey jacket, grey sweater, grey trousers, and, for all I know, grey undergarments, he addresses his youthful charges in a nasal bleat that makes George McGovern sound like Macho Man by comparison. Since he also dubs voice-overs for all of the puppet characters, the aural impression, like his personal color scheme, is uniformly bland. The premise of the show, shaped in part by two "psychological consultants" whose names are run with the credits, seems to be that hyperactive young Americans need nothing so much as a daily aerial lobotomy, presided over by the unmenacing May-Bap figure embodying the virtues of a kindly granddad and a particularly unassertive schoolmarm. . . . By the time Mr. Rogers discards his tennis shoes and sweater and heads for the door at the end of each thirty-minute installment, one can't help suspecting that the brighter kids in the audience breathe a sigh of relief refreshed with the certainty that, for a merciful 24-hour interlude, "Mr. Rogers' Neighborhood" has gone with the wimp.[2]

With a few minor changes, Mr. Bakshian's comments about Mr. Rogers could be the comments of the average pagan talking about a Christian. The stereotype the world has given to Christians is nothing less than frightening. When anyone becomes a Christian, given that stereotype, it is even more a miracle of God's grace than the Bible says it is.

A young couple came to see me once with a request that I perform their marriage ceremony. There was a problem. She was a Christian, and he was not and had no interest in becoming one. I explained to them that the Bible placed on me a certain obligation about the kinds of couples for whom I could perform the marriage ceremony. I told them that I could marry two Christians and I could marry two pagans, but that I couldn't "cross-fertilize" (see 2 Cor. 6:14–15). And so I explained to them that I was prevented from performing the ceremony.

Then to my horror, the young woman began to cry. If that was upsetting to me, you should have seen her fiancé. This big, bad pastor had hurt his future wife, and he was really ticked. He rose up to his full six feet three and clenched his fists and said, "Reverend, I thought the church was here to help people; I thought you were here to keep people from crying, not to make them cry." And then he took his future wife's hand and pulled her out the door. (To be perfectly honest with you, I was glad to see them go. He was mad and he was big. I'm not a wimp, but I'm not stupid either.)

I was thinking about that incident later, and I decided that his view of the church, though obviously wrong from a biblical standpoint, was nevertheless the view held by many people. If they don't hate us, they think that we are a relatively benign institution set apart to "hatch, match, and dispatch." It is no wonder that as Christians become involved politically there are such loud protests. Norman Lear thought there was a pet kitten over in the corner, and the kitten turned out to be a lion. When a kitten roars like a lion, has claws like a lion, and has teeth like a lion, you don't want him on your lap—you want him in a cage.

Not too long ago I was in a meeting between the editors of our local newspaper and the religious leaders in the community. It was a meeting designed to help us understand each other. One of the editors, who was trying to explain the newspaper's position, said, "We don't go after the church in a news story unless the church does something outside its traditional role."

I was angry, and before I had a chance to put on my smiling clergy face, I was talking. "Are you telling us," I said, "that you will leave us alone as long as we keep our place, but if we do something that doesn't fit your preconceived idea of what the church does, we will not be okay?"

To be perfectly honest with you, his words sounded to me like the words of a racist telling blacks that as long as they dance, sing, play the trumpet, eat watermelon, and keep their place, they will be okay. The editor, of course, denied that that was what he meant, but I have no doubt that his "Freudian slip" was showing.

I believe that Jerry Falwell and many like him are hated, not only for the things for which they stand, but because they aren't supposed to stand at all. They are Christians, and Christians are supposed to be seen and not heard; Christians are supposed to stay in church, smile, and talk about God; Christians are supposed to bless the mess of paganism and act like a kept woman.

Unless you have been hiding under a rock somewhere, you are aware of the unfortunate stereotype of Christians in our society. It is the stereotype that files Christians under the heading "Wimp."

WHAT WE THINK OF OURSELVES

The wimp stereotype makes me angry, but let me tell you something that makes me sad: We Christians have often been the ones to create the stereotype and we have then tried to conform to it. In other words, the horrible thing is that in some ways the world's pathetic stereotype of us is the same as our stereotype of ourselves.

It is important what the world thinks about us, but far more important is what we think about ourselves. In the chapters that follow, I am not too concerned with what the world thinks about Christians. I am, however, very much concerned with what we think about ourselves.

Someone tells the story of the eagle egg that somehow got into a chicken coop. The mother hen realized the egg was somewhat larger than the other eggs, but after all, she was a mother so she sat on it. The eagle hatched and for weeks played the chicken game. The eagle knew he was different; he knew that the other chickens thought he was different and they only tolerated him. He tried to eat off the floor of the chicken coop like the other chickens, but it never felt right. He tried to walk like a chicken and talk like a chicken and squawk like a chicken, but he could never quite pull it off.

Sometimes the eagle would look up in the sky and wonder what was on the other side of the clouds. He would say to his fellow chickens, "Don't you ever wonder what's up there in the sky or what's on the other side of the mountains?" The other chickens would look at him as if his elevator didn't go all the way to the top. But he never stopped wondering and asking questions.

Then one day the eagle looked up in the sky and saw a speck. The speck grew larger and larger until the eagle realized that it was a creature like himself, an eagle. He heard the creature call loudly, and the call echoed against the chicken coop. At that moment the eagle knew he wasn't a chicken. He knew he was an eagle. He flapped his wings and began to fly, and soon he was soaring above the clouds.

The problem with that eagle wasn't just that everyone thought he was a chicken. His real problem was that *he* thought he was a chicken. Something like that has happened to Christians. Somehow we have gotten the idea that being a Christian means being a wimp. It isn't true, but if enough people tell you that you are a wimp, you'll start acting like one. That can be overcome if you know the truth. If you don't know the truth, however, you can end up staying in the chicken coop the rest of your life.

In the next chapter I want to talk to you about what the Bible says we are. Before we do that, let's take a moment and talk about the development of the stereotype among Christians themselves. It is my thesis that Christian boldness doesn't happen because we don't believe that Christian boldness *should* happen.

Let me give you some Scripture that is important to this discussion. The first passage is found in Proverbs 23:7, where the writer admonished believers to stay away from certain people because "as he thinks in his heart, so is he." Philippians 4:8 says, "Finally, brethren, whatever things are true, whatever things are noble, whatever things are just, whatever things are pure, whatever things are lovely, whatever things are of good report, if there is any virtue and if there is anything praiseworthy—meditate on these things." The psalmist, when he asked God to "check him out," said, "Search me, O God, and know my heart" (Ps. 139:23). And Paul, in telling the Christians at Rome to be transformed, said, "Be transformed by the renewing of your mind, that you may prove what is that good and acceptable and perfect will of God" (Rom. 12:2b).

The point is this: What we think about the world, and especially what we think about ourselves, will inform and mold our actions. If Christians think that being a Christian means being weak, insipid, and bland, then we will be weak, insipid, and bland. Not only that, but if enough of us think it, we will give the impression both to the world and to those who have just become believers that Christianity is weak, insipid, and bland. Eventually (and this is the great concern of this book), the lie will become the reality.

Everything I will be writing in this book will be wasted unless there is a way to put it into practice. How does one deal with a bad stereotype within oneself? I want to give you an important biblical principle, and then I want to draw three implications from that principle.

THE PRINCIPLE OF CONTROL

The principle is called the principle of control, and it works like this: *Your mind controls your actions and emotions; your will controls your mind; you control your will. Therefore, you control your actions and your emotions.* When the Bible tells Christians to "think about these things," it presupposes that you have decided or, at minimum, *can* decide to think about them. The reason the Bible is so insistent on thinking about certain things or renewing your mind is that your mind and the attendant thinking process are the very center of everything you will become.

I spend most of my life on airplanes, and flying is my second favorite activity in the world (the first being to jump off buildings). At any rate, a few months ago a friend who has a private plane was taking me to a speaking engagement. Once we were up and flying, he took his hands off the controls and said, "Steve, it's all yours." I just about died.

"Jim," I said, "unless you are prepared to meet thy God, you had better take control of this thing. I refuse to touch it." My problem was that he gave me control and I didn't want it.

A lot of us are like that about life. We really don't want the responsibility for control. Mary McCarthy has said, "Bureaucracy, the rule of no one, has become the modern form of despotism." We don't like to be in control, because we don't like to be responsible. I believe the reason we have committees is that nobody wants to make decisions, take control, and be responsible. So we spread it around. But the point is that you can't escape responsibility at least for what you think and what you do. Your mind controls your actions and emotions; your will controls your mind; you control your will. Therefore, you control your actions and your emotions.

You Are What You've Decided to Be

Now, let's draw some implications from the principle. First, you are, at this moment, what you have decided to be. When Joshua renewed the covenant of the people with God at Shechem, he said, "And if it seems evil to you to serve the LORD, choose for yourselves this day whom you will serve . . ." (Josh. 24:15a).

We live in an age in which perverted psychology has reduced people to the status of computers. If a person has not been programmed properly, we are told, he will manifest aberrant behavior. He is not responsible for what he does; he has no choice but to act as he has been programmed. The need, psychologists will say, is to take a "sick" person and simply reprogram.

That approach would just be silly except that people have come to believe that whatever they are really is the result of how they were "potty trained" or of the self-image given to them by their parents. Murderers are not bad people; they are maladjusted people. Child molesters aren't to be punished; they are to be understood. Thieves have not done anything wrong; they simply have a correctable psychological problem.

Someone tells about a man who was sitting on a tack, and it was hurting. A psychologist came along and said, "Sir, the reason you are hurting is rooted in a childhood trauma. You need therapy." A sociologist then came along, saw the hurting man, and said, "You've got a problem, and it is obviously the result of the kind of environment in which you grew up. Hurt is from an improper environment." An economist next came along and said, "Money is the root of all hurt. Let me help you with your portfolio." Then a minister came along and said, "If you learn to praise the Lord in all your circumstances, you won't hurt so much. Your spiritual life leaves something to be desired. Start reading your Bible and praying every day, and it will get better." Finally a little girl came along and said, "Mister, why don't you get off the tack?"

One of the great discoveries of my life as a pastor who counsels was the discovery that people are what they have decided to be. We do things for what seem to us, either consciously or unconsciously, to be perfectly logical reasons. Most of the time when someone is depressed, that person has decided to be depressed. If someone is a "pain in the neck," most of the time that person has decided to be a "pain in the neck." With few exceptions, we are what we have decided to be. People are not computers. We are volitional beings; we make choices; those choices determine what we become.

You Can Change

The second implication of the principle of control is this: Not only are you what you have decided to be, but you can also be different from what you are. Recently I was talking to a young man who said he came to me because he needed help. He told me he had some friends who had become a bad influence in his life. They liked to go to a particular club where there were plenty of drugs, and even though he had promised himself and God that he wouldn't do it anymore, he couldn't help going there with his friends. He said he had tried everything, but nothing seemed to give him the strength he needed to stop going with his friends to this particular place and participating with them in taking drugs. He expected me to give him some Scripture or some magic formula that would help him.

I said simply, "Son, why don't you stop?"

"I can't," he replied.

"What do you mean you can't stop? You're the one who goes there. Nobody forces you. You're the one who takes the drugs. Nobody puts a gun to your head and makes you take them. So just stop."

The young man smiled and said, "You know, nobody ever put it to me that way."

Three weeks later the young man called and said, "Pastor, you gave me the best advice I have ever received. You said stop and I did. I haven't touched drugs since I talked to you."

Now that may seem silly to you. You thought pastors had some kind of secret formula. You thought we could pray over problems and they would go away. But as silly as it sounds, that young man had not heard from anybody the simple advice that he should stop the bad things he was doing. Twenty years ago, I would not have had to tell him he should stop. Everybody knew that we decide what we are and are what we have decided. It is an indication of how far our society has come down the road of complete helplessness that I had to tell him to make a choice. (I do not mean by using this example to minimize the difficulty of breaking a serious drug addiction. But in that situation, too, the person must begin by making a basic choice to stop using the drug, even if following through is painful or requires the help of others.)

As you read this book, it is my hope that you will get some insights that will help you understand what the Bible really says about insipid Christianity. It is my hope that you will want to change. You can!

What You Decide Affects Your Relationship with God

The third implication one can draw from the principle of control is this: What you decide will determine the reality and the peace of God in your life. Paul, after telling his friends in Philippi to think about certain things because it could make a difference, makes a very interesting statement: "The things which you learned and received and heard and saw in me, these do, and the God of peace will be with you" (Phil. 4:9).

There is a strange paradox I have discovered in my life, and I'll bet you have discovered it too. When I am too frightened to make waves for Christ, when I have chosen to go over in a corner and avoid conflict and problems, when I have chosen to take the easy way out, and when I have chosen to allow my faith to be insipid, I find that my anxiety level rises. In fact, that which I think will lessen my worry and anxiety does just the opposite. However, I have found that when I stand, God stands with me.

In Acts 5, you will remember, the apostles are in prison for standing for Christ, but "at night an angel of the Lord opened the prison doors and brought them out" (Acts 5:19). When was the last time you saw an angel? Probably it's been a long time, if ever. Let me ask you another question: When was the last time you were in prison? If we went to prison more, we would see more angels.

In the second book of C. S. Lewis's science fiction trilogy, *Perelandra*, Ransom had been sent to Perelandra to prevent a fall similar to the one that ruined Adam on earth. The adversary, in the form of a man named Weston, was also on Perelandra working against Ransom and his efforts to prevent another great tragedy. Ransom realized with horror the evil represented by Weston and gradually came to understand that he must face and destroy Weston. It was a frightening prospect. In the darkness of the Perelandran night, Ransom considered the fact that he could stand and fight or he could run. Out of the blackness a voice rang, "My name is also Ransom."[3]

The point is this: Our efforts to obtain peace by slinking off quietly into a corner, trying to stay out of the way of any problem or conflict, and keeping our mouths shut are fruitless. In fact, the best way to find peace is to stand boldly for Christ, because if you stand, He will stand with you.

All right, now it is time to get down to business, and our business is shattering the pagan's stereotype of the Christian as a bland, insipid wimp. But before we can do that, we must shatter our own stereotype. That won't be easy; both the pagans and the Christians have been working on the stereotype for a long time.

In the remaining chapters I want to give you knowledge and principles. But that, as much as it is, is not enough. God has to grant us His grace. Our prayer ought to be the prayer of the sea captain in the middle of a hurricane: "O God, help us, and come Yourself because this ain't no time for boys."

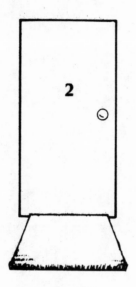

"The wicked flee when no one pursues, but the righteous are bold as a lion."

PROVERBS 28:1

God
Don't Make No
Wimps

2

One of the difficult tasks facing the person who has decided to be a bold Christian is the challenge he or she has in finding models for boldness. It isn't that there are no models; those models abound. The problem is that our culture (the church included) has a false idea of what a Christian ought to be. We have gone to the Bible and to the church history books with that preconceived idea in mind, and reality has suffered. In other words, we have emasculated the record. Time after time the earthy men and women of our past have come out looking like nice, middle-class ladies and gentlemen who have been commissioned by God to make the world nice. It is enough to make one blush.

Not too long ago I was at an ecclesiastical meeting and during lunch sat down at a table where some rather vocal feminists were discussing their feelings on the rearing of children. One of the women said that she was against guns, and that she had decided the only toys she was going to give her son were dolls.

The other women agreed, and one woman said that she had not only taken the toy guns away from her two sons, but had also forbidden them to be involved in competitive sports. She said, "I feel that aggression, no matter what form it takes, is the result of training, and I am going to train my children to be different."

I'm not in the business of making a case for toy guns and competitive sports. (In fact, if I had sons I'm not sure how I would train them in those areas. God, having blessed me with two daughters, only sends boys to men who need help.) I was, however, depressed after that lunch. I felt sorry for those boys because they were being brought up with a false view of reality. I got the distinct impression that the reality they were going to be taught would be the they-would-be-nice-to-you-if-you-will-be-nice-to-them reality. I was afraid they were going to be taught about a world where all differences can be resolved calmly and rationally, a world where nice people sit down and talk out their problems. I feared they were going to be given the false idea that when others see how nice we are, they will want to be Christians too. That, it seems to me, was bad enough, but when you add the fact that the false view of reality was being taught to those boys in the name of Christianity, you have a very serious problem. When they grow up, I hope someone tells them the truth. If they don't hear the truth, they will end up either fitting the mold of "nice Christianity" or they will leave the faith altogether, thinking that Christianity simply isn't viable.

One sometimes gets the feeling that Christians stand against war, or abortion, or pornography because those things are not "nice." May God have mercy on us if the blood of Christ was shed and the only result is niceness. I am reminded of H. Richard Niebuhr's comment about modern Christianity and its theology of "a God without wrath who brought men without sin into a kingdom without judgment through the ministrations of a

Christ without a cross." The Christian faith recognizes the aggressiveness of the world. It creates heroes and heroines who will not bend, break, or compromise. It teaches that there is a lusty, materialistic paganism out to eat us alive unless we find something better than pious platitudes and nice news.

THE MEN AND WOMEN OF THE BIBLE

Let's look at the record. If you take the time to examine that record without any preconceived ideas, you become acutely aware that most of the men and women of the Bible and church history would be uncomfortable with our bland religion. Abraham, Isaac, and Jacob would wince to see what we have done with what they started. Moses would get angry enough to find some stone tablets to break. Joshua might call out his fearless and godly troops and fight to give the land back to the pagans. Gideon, Deborah, and Samson would wonder who was leading, and the prophets would laugh. John the Baptist would never get invited to dinner—and would be glad. Peter would wonder where the Christians went. Priscilla and Lydia would make jokes about the silly, costless Christianity they saw, and Paul would blush. And God, who wants His people to be far more earthy, bold, and real than the pagans, must find that the cross at the center of His heart hurts more than it did before.

The first miracle Jesus performed was at a wedding party. You will remember that Jesus on that occasion turned the water into wine (see John 2). Someone has suggested that modern day Christianity has been busy turning the wine back into water. That is true. We have taken what was a very real and exciting gift, and we have made it into something so bland that most of the people who first received the gift wouldn't be able to recognize it.

There is a story about a man who ordered plans from a certain company to build a birdhouse. He thought it would look nice in his back yard, and he liked birds. When the plans arrived and he tried to make the birdhouse, he discovered that a mistake had been made and the company had sent him plans for a sailboat. He wrote to the company explaining the problem, and they wrote back a letter of apology. They explained that his request had gotten mixed up with some other requests, and that they would correct the error. In the last line of the letter, the company representative said, "However, if you think you had problems with your birdhouse, you ought to see the man who ordered the plans for a sailboat. He says that his new boat looks funny and that it won't float."

Somebody has gotten the plans mixed up! Too many Christians are trying to sail around in birdhouses that have been built using the wrong plans. It is important, it seems to me, to get the copy of the original plans and then start from scratch with the construction. The questions before building the house are these: What did God intend for Christians? Is weakness a part of the original plan? Is *insipid* a synonym for *love*? Is it possible to be bold and Christian at the same time? Can Christians continue to follow Christ and at the same time be strong, clear, and bold? As we check out the plan, we might be surprised at what we find.

In Exodus 34 Moses renewed the covenant with the people of God. If you remember, Moses had been up on the mountain receiving the law of God. Meanwhile, back on the ranch, Aaron and the people had made a golden idol and had fallen down and worshiped it. When Moses got down from the mountain and found out what was happening, he didn't go off in a corner and whine. He didn't cry out, "Mercy teacups!" He didn't talk about love and forgiveness. He got angry— really angry. There are a number of disconcerting things that happened as a result of the idol worship of the Israelites, but eventually God renewed the covenant with His people. Among other things God said to Moses, He said this: "Behold, I make a covenant. Before all your people I will do marvels such as have not been done in all the earth, nor in any nation; and all the people among whom you are shall see the work of the LORD. For it is an awesome thing that I will do with you" (Exod. 34:10).

"An awesome thing" God does with His people. When was the last time you heard the word *awesome* used to describe the people of God and what He had done with them? I don't know about you, but I haven't heard that word used in a long, long time.

As you read through the Scripture, you find sinful men and women, dishonest men and women, fearful men and women—but you do not find weak men and women. In fact, over and over one sees that a relationship with the God of the universe makes people "awesome."

Consider Joshua, the great fighter for God. When he was called, it was because a man he loved and followed had died. One would expect that Joshua would simply fall apart. But he didn't! Listen to what God said to Joshua:

> Moses My servant is dead. Now therefore, arise, go over this Jordan, you and all this people, to the land which I am giving to them—the children of Israel. Every place that the sole of your foot will tread upon I have given you, as I said to Moses. From the wilderness and this Lebanon as far as the great river, the River Euphrates, all the land of the Hittites, and to the Great Sea toward the going down of the sun, shall be your territory. No man shall be able to stand before you all the days of your life; as I was with Moses, so I will be with you. I will not leave you nor forsake you. *Be strong and of good courage. . .* (Josh. 1:2–6a, italics mine).

Thereupon follows a story of courage, strength, and commitment. Nobody laughed at Joshua.

Just open your Old Testament and take a cursory look at the judges of Israel. They march across the pages of Scripture leaving fire in their wake. If you are looking for weak and insipid folks, don't look at Deborah, Othniel, Gideon, or Samson. And then consider the last judge, Samuel. When he spoke, people listened because "all Israel from Dan to Beersheba knew that Samuel had been established as a prophet of the LORD" (1 Sam. 3:20). How did they know? They didn't know because he was soft and gentle. They knew because God's power was clear in his life.

Consider David. David was not always good, but he was strong. "So David went on and became great, and the LORD God of hosts was with him" (2 Sam. 5:10). David's greatness was again because his God made him strong.

While we're making the list, let's not forget to include Elijah on Mount Carmel. One man, God's man, against four hundred and fifty prophets of Baal. Read the story in I Kings 18. Look at Elijah's making fun of the prophets of Baal when their god didn't bother to answer their prayers. "Cry aloud, for he is a god; either he is meditating, or he is busy, or he is on a journey, or perhaps he is sleeping and must be awakened" (v. 27). Today many people would judge Elijah as being intolerant and arrogant. God judged him as being faithful.

While you are making the list, be sure to include Shadrach, Meshach, and Abednego from the book of Daniel. You will remember that they were three young men who refused to bow down before Nebuchadnezzar's image. The Scripture says that Nebuchadnezzar reacted with "rage and fury." He then asked the three if their God was going to protect them in the fiery furnace to which they were going if they didn't bow down. He pointed out that they were going to die for their convictions. The boldness of their reply is almost astounding: "O Nebuchadnezzar, we have no need to answer you in this matter. If that is the case, our God whom we serve is able to deliver us from the burning fiery furnace, and He will deliver us from your hand, O king. But if not, let it be known to you, O king, that we do not serve your gods, nor will we worship the gold image which you have set up" (Dan. 3:16–18).

Don't leave Ezra and Nehemiah out of the list either. They were builders, fighters, and leaders. Against overwhelming odds they were willing to stand up and be counted. While we are talking about strong leaders, stop and take a look at the prophets. They all needed a course in tact. As we read their words, it is enough to make us wince. Listen to Amos speaking the word of God:

> I hate, I despise your feast days, And I do not savor your sacred assemblies. Though you offer Me burnt offerings and your grain offerings, I will not accept them, nor will I regard your fattened peace offerings. Take away from Me the noise of your songs, For I will not hear the melody of your stringed instruments. But let justice run down like water, And righteousness like a mighty stream (Amos 5:21–24).

The prophets would be uncomfortable in the company of nice Christians.

The New Testament will not yield any models for our soft and insipid kind of Christianity either. Can you imagine John the Baptist as a part of the evangelical jet set? His clothes simply would not fit in with the well-dressed clergyman's image. His voice thundered judgment, his demeanor frightened, and his food was locusts. No, John the Baptist just won't do. Peter, the rock; James and John, the sons of thunder; Paul, the bold rabbi—all of them were gutsy Christians who made the world tremble. Listen to the sarcasm of Paul to the people at Corinth:

> Now I, Paul, myself am pleading with you by the meekness and gentleness of Christ—who in presence am lowly among you, but being absent am bold toward you [evidently a quote from one of his enemies from Corinth]. But I beg you that when I am present I may not be bold with that confidence by which I intend to be bold against some, who think of us as if we walked according to the flesh (2 Cor. 10:1–2).

You won't find Jesus as the model of weakness. What we have done to Him has been a crime. We have made Him nice and sweet . . . and He isn't. He was gentle, but his gentleness was only a part of the picture. Listen to His words:

> Woe to you, scribes and Pharisees, hypocrites! For you are like whitewashed tombs which indeed appear beautiful outwardly, but inside are full of dead men's bones and all uncleanness. Even so you also outwardly appear righteous to men, but inside you are full of hypocrisy and lawlessness. Woe to you, scribes and Pharisees, hypocrites! Because you build the tombs of the

prophets and adorn the monuments of the righteous, and say, "If we had lived in the days of our fathers, we would not have been partakers with them in the blood of the prophets." Therefore you are witnesses against yourselves that you are sons of those who murdered the prophets. Fill up, then, the measure of your fathers' guilt. Serpents, brood of vipers! How can you escape the condemnation of hell? (Matt. 23:27–33).

Do those sound like the words of a wimp? Can you imagine a dear saint telling Jesus, as he braids the whip and prepares to enter the temple to overthrow the moneychangers, "Now, Jesus, be nice"?

Wherever we got our idea of the Christian as a sweet servant, we certainly didn't get it from the Bible. We didn't get it from church history either.

EXAMPLES FROM CHURCH HISTORY

As you look through the history of the church of Christ since the first century, you will find that the men and women who gave us our heritage were also strong, earthy, committed, bold Christians. Those people haunt my dreams and capture my imagination. Sometimes when I close my eyes at night, I can hear the cries of the martyrs and the curses of the adversaries. I can picture the parade of men and women who have stood up to the world without bending, breaking, or compromising.

I can see Irenaeus during the last quarter of the second century serving as Bishop of Lyons where his predecessor, Pothinus, died at the hand of Marcus Aurelius. His strength and power turned almost an entire population to Christ, and his most famous work *Against All Heresies* was a bold statement defending the Christian faith against all comers.

Or I think of Origen (C.A.D. 185–c.254), who watched his father, Leonidas, die for his faith in Christ and who stood strong and bold for the rest of his life only to face torture and finally death at the hands of those who could not abide his courageous strength.

Chrysostom (A.D. 347–407) attacked every social and spiritual evil of his time and for his boldness was sent into exile, where he died broken in body but not in spirit. Augustine (A.D. 354–430), a contemporary of Chrysostom, was one of the most earthy Christians Jesus ever called. When told of the fall of Rome, he was sad but commented to the effect that while he was a citizen of Rome, he was also a citizen of a city that would never fall. You can read about it in his book *City of God*.

Listen to some of Augustine's "soft" words spoken to those who had been spared in the fall of Rome because they called themselves Christians:

> Therefore ought they to give God thanks, and with sincere confession flee for refuge to His name, that so they may escape the punishment of eternal fire—they who with lying lips took upon them this name, that they might escape the punishment of present destruction. For of those whom you see insolently and shamelessly insulting the servants of Christ, there are numbers who would not have escaped that destruction and slaughter had they not pretended that they themselves were Christ's servants. Yet now, in ungrateful pride and most impious madness, and at the risk of being punished in everlasting darkness, they perversely oppose that name under which they fraudulently protected themselves for the sake of enjoying the light of this brief life.[1]

The sermons of Bernard of Clairvaux (A.D. 1090–1153) ought to be read by every Christian who thinks that "sweet" and "Christian" go together. One biographer of Bernard said of him, "Bernard was a man of humility, but one who spoke with great conviction when convinced that he was right; he never apologized for his message."[2]

The list grows long and the space is limited, but we must not forget Luther standing at Worms. His message was certainly not your typical let's-be-friends-and-love-Jesus appeal. He said, when asked to recant on penalty of excommunication, "Here I stand, I can do no other, so help me God." And then there is John Knox railing at Queen Mary, and the queen crying out in desperation, "I fear the prayers of John Knox more than an army of ten thousand men." You can see in John Knox a passion that many modern-day Christians would find offensive. He cried, "Oh God, give me Scotland or I die."

I think of Peter Cartwright, an early American Methodist pioneer preacher. It is said that when he approached a town, he would often stand on a hill above the town and those with him would hear him say, "I smell hell!" Such language! I fear that today we would stand on the same hill and talk about the beautiful flowers and trees that God has made.

Our past is ripe with models of strength, boldness, and courage. Gregory, Theodora, Savonarola, Beza, Ridley, Latimer, Zwingli, Wesley, Whitfield, Zinzendorf, the Countess of Huntingdon, Newton, Edwards, Mather, and Moody all walk in my dreams. Sometimes I can hear the scorn and the Scripture falling from the lips of the Scottish Covenanters and the French Huguenots as they went to their deaths. In my dreams I hear the crackle of the flames and the blows of the hammers as they went home to be with Christ.

Revivalist Billy Sunday's words, while perhaps not as eloquent as Spurgeon's or as deep as Calvin's, ring out over the heritage of the church: "I'm against sin. I'll kick it as long as I've got a foot, and I'll fight it as long as I've got a fist. I'll butt it as long as I've got a head. I'll bite it as long as I've got a tooth. When I'm old and fistless and footless and toothless, I'll gum it till I go home to glory and it goes home to perdition!"

I've left out so much in our list, but there is enough here to let you know that our heritage has been sold for a mess of pottage. There is enough to remind us that God, at least in the past, has not been in the business of creating wimps. Given the fact that He doesn't change His mind, it is easy to construct a syllogism. Premise: God has not, in the past, created wimps. Premise: God doesn't change His mind. Conclusion: God isn't creating wimps now.

THE IMPORTANCE OF DEFINITION

Somehow Christians have gotten the idea that when God speaks of love, He is speaking of something some dreamer wrote a song about—not biblical love.

In C. S. Lewis's *The Great Divorce*, a man encountered a shining lady who turns out to be his wife. The man (referred to as the Tragedian or the Dwarf) was on his way to hell, and she was trying to get him to heaven. There is a great dialogue between the two.

> "Darling," said the Lady to the Dwarf, "there's nothing to face. You don't want me to have been miserable for misery's sake. You only think I must have been if I loved you. But if you'll only wait you'll see that it isn't so."
>
> "Love!" said the Tragedian striking his forehead with his hand: then, a few notes deeper, "Love! Do you know the meaning of the word?"
>
> "How should I not?" said the Lady. "I am in love. In love, do you understand? Yes, now I love truly."
>
> "You mean," said the Tragedian, "you mean—you did not love me truly in the old days?"
>
> "Only in a poor sort of way," she answered. "I have asked you to forgive me. There was a little real love in it. But what we called love down there was mostly the craving to be loved. In the main I loved you for my own sake: because I needed you. . . . What needs could I have now that I have all? I am full now, not empty. I am in Love Himself, not lonely. Strong, not weak. You shall be the same. Come and see. We shall have no need for one another now: we can begin to love truly."[3]

The Bible (and also church history) is a great love story. We have always understood that, but the problem was that we allowed the world to define love for us. Definition, however, must come from truth, not vice versa. The rest of this book is about definition. God doesn't make wimps. We think He does because we have defined love in those terms and then taken that definition back to the source, the Bible, and tried to read it in terms of our own definition.

Four Principles of Definition

Let me give you four principles that are very important. The first is this: Biblical definition precludes tragedy. In other words, we must know who we are in order to know how to function. If we function in a manner divergent from the truth, we will end up in tragic situations; if we live consistently with what the Bible teaches, we can avoid those tragedies.

You don't have to be a Christian very long before some pagan tells you that the Christian faith produces people with a bad self-image. They usually say something like this: "You are always saying that people are sinners, and that is the road to creating a bad self-image."

Now let me tell you the truth. The way to create a bad self-image is to build your self-image on a lie. If I tell you that I'm okay and you're okay when in fact neither of us is, we are headed for some very difficult situations. (Someone has said that Jesus said from the cross, "If I'm okay and you're okay, what in the world are you doing down there, and what in the world am I doing up here?") The best way to create a good, healthy self-image is to be honest about self-definition. I would like to sing, but I can't sing. If someone tells me I am a wonderful singer, and I stand in front of an audience and sing, I am going to make a fool of myself. The point is this: Biblical definition precludes tragedy. Conversely, ignoring biblical definition *produces* tragedy.

The second principle is this: Biblical definition places value. I think it was Leighton Ford who told about a prostitute's approaching a missionary. The missionary asked her her price, and she told him. The missionary then said, "Dear, that is not even close to enough. You are worth much more than that." And then he told her about Christ.

It is terribly important that we remember our value. The reason we are often weak and cowardly is that we have not defined ourselves in terms of what the Bible says. A man observed a nurse during a war as she did the kind of dirty work nurses do, and he was amazed at her ability. He said to her, "Sister, I wouldn't do that for a million dollars."

She replied, "Brother, I wouldn't do this for a million dollars either."

What she was saying is that she didn't have to do that kind of work; she was a volunteer acting out of commitment, not necessity. She had defined herself properly.

Principle number three: Biblical definition precipitates contentment. Did you know that studies have shown it is almost impossible to give a dog an ulcer? Do you know why? Because dogs hardly ever try to be anything but a dog. You can say a lot of bad things about a dog, but a dog never tries to be something else. That is a wonderful, redeeming quality.

I used to watch the women walking their dogs on Boston Common, and sometimes in the dead of winter some of the dogs would be dressed as human beings—sweater, booties, and nose warmer. Sometimes those dogs would look at me as if to say, "I know it looks foolish, but she makes me wear this stuff. Would you talk to her for me?"

Dogs are always dogs; they never try to be something they aren't. If we were better defined and accepted what God has called us to be, we would have fewer ulcers. The problem is that when Christians finally decide to be bold about their witness and about life, they feel guilty. Why? Because they think they are doing something wrong. That discontent can be remedied by a simple but life-changing application of biblical truth.

And then the final principle: Biblical definition also precedes action. This principle is a correlation of the last principle and simply teaches that when you know who you are, you know what you are supposed to do. I served as a pastor for years before I found out what the biblical definition of a pastor was. Let me tell you something: If you are a pastor and you don't know God, you have a great job. I played golf, went fishing, and had a grand old time—until I found out what the Bible said about pastors. All of a sudden my role became clear, and I knew what I was supposed to do.

The problem with most weak Christians is that they need to be defined. You are a child of the King of the universe. If you stand around whining about how terrible you are, if you allow the world's definition to stand, it will develop into neurosis, and that will make you weak and insipid. For God's sake, go to the Bible for your definition. For God's sake, look at what God has done among His people for the last three thousand years. For God's sake, allow Him to tell you who you are.

I think it was Hugh Latimer's wife who said to him, just before he was to go before Queen ("Bloody") Mary, "Now dear, don't you shilly shally!" She was speaking the word of God.

He says to His people: "Now, don't you shilly shally. I don't make wimps."

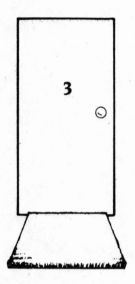

"Have I not commanded you? Be strong and of good courage; do not be afraid, nor be dismayed, for the LORD your God is with you."

JOSHUA 1:9

Freedom for the Father

3

One of the good things about working on a book is that in the process you find yourself changing. If it is a good book and it is faithful to the Scriptures, the change is usually for the better. One of the reasons I write is that I expect there to be positive change on my part and the part of the reader as a result. This book, because of its nature, is written with an even higher expectation of change.

There are some very real dangers in change, however, especially when that change is in the direction of boldness. In the next chapter I want to talk to you about some of the risk involved. But now I want to turn to the danger of becoming something God never intended.

We have all heard such platitudinous wisdom as "a rose by any other name" and "if it walks like a duck, looks like a duck, and quacks like a duck, it must be a duck." Most of the time when you look at a rose, you can call it anything you like, but it is still a rose. And when you come across anything that looks, walks, and quacks like a duck, it usually is a duck. But not always. Let's talk about exceptions.

COUNTERFEIT FREEDOM AND JOY

Someone has said that Satan will use 99 percent of the truth to float one lie. That is correct, and because it is, it is terribly important that we Christians be careful as to how we assess new religions, new believers, new doctrines, and new books—even this one.

I remember the day that I found myself free. I didn't have to please everybody; I didn't have to be Billy Graham; I didn't have to be guilty all the time; I didn't have to smile at everybody; I didn't have to come up to everybody's expectations of me; I didn't have to be a kind, nice, sweet pastor. I felt as if the world had been lifted off my shoulders. I could cry out with the slave after emancipation: "I'm free! I'm free! Praise God Almighty, I'm free at last!"

Now, the problem with the freedom and the joy I feel is that there are many others who express the same freedom and joy—and they are not Christians. I have heard graduates of EST, adherents to the principles of Scientology and Transcendental Meditation, and people who have had a "numinous" encounter with God all express a similar experience. That used to bother me a great deal. Because they talked about freedom and joy, did it mean they had the same source? Was God the center of a spoked wheel, and, like the spokes, were there many different ways to Him? Did we all, at the center of things, really believe the same thing? Did it matter what one believed as long as one was sincere about it?

Professor William Kilpatrick, in his very good book *Psychological Seduction*, speaks about the necessity of having something better to offer others than an experience. He said:

> I sometimes ask my students, many of whom look forward to careers in the helping professions, what they will have to offer—say, to the alcoholic—that's better than "god in a bottle." Their answers tend to be framed along psychological lines: "adjustment to society," "coping," "a better self-concept," and so

forth. Those responses, it seems to me, miss the point. If you can have god in a bottle, and temporarily be a god yourself, why would you settle for such paltry things as adjustment or coping? Once you have tasted transcendence, even the spurious kind, it is no easy matter to come back to earth.[1]

The question is this: What is the difference between my experience and the experience of others if we describe the experience in the same way? If someone can find freedom and joy in a bottle, what is the difference between my freedom and joy and his? The difference is in the source of the experience and in the truth that comes from it.

Most believers don't realize there is a counterfeit to almost everything God does in the believer's life. A counterfeit is not the real thing, but it is close enough to be passed off to the unwary as real. That is why one must be very careful to judge "experience" on the basis of the truth of Scripture, and not on the existence of experience itself. "Now the Spirit expressly says that in latter times some will depart from the faith, giving heed to deceiving spirits and doctrines of demons" (1 Tim. 4:1). This point is also clearly made in 1 John 4:1–3:

> Beloved, do not believe every spirit, but test the spirits, whether they are of God; because many false prophets have gone out into the world. By this you know the Spirit of God: Every spirit that confesses that Jesus Christ has come in the flesh is of God, and every spirit that does not confess that Jesus Christ has come in the flesh is not of God. And this is the spirit of the Antichrist, which you have heard was coming, and is now already in the world.

The reason I am saying all this is to attach a very important warning to everything that is said in this book: All boldness is not Christian boldness. Or to put it another way: Just because you are bold does not mean that you are Christian. It may simply mean that you have a "mean streak."

It is not my desire to see Christians becoming narrow, negative, and abrasive. I do think the boldness that comes from Christ may make you more narrow than you are now; it may enable you to say no more often; it may make you more confrontational than you are now. But it is terribly important that you understand the difference between what comes from God and what is simply a selfish need to control and intimidate others.

And so I want to show you the difference between Christian boldness and the boldness that comes from the teachings of, say, a Wayne Dyer or a Hobart Mowrer. There will be certain parallels, of course, but there are significant differences. If it looks, walks, and quacks like a duck—it just may not be a duck.

THE UNIQUENESS OF CHRISTIAN BOLDNESS

What then is the difference between Christian boldness and "pulling your own strings," "looking out for number one," or "winning through intimidation"? In other words, what makes Christian boldness different from "pagan" boldness?

A key verse for this discussion is found in Paul's second letter to his young friend Timothy. Paul said, "For God has not given us a spirit of fear, but of power and of love and of a sound mind" (2 Timothy 1:7). And so, from the Scripture, there are four distinguishing marks of Christian boldness. Let's check them out.

Christian Boldness Is Courageous

First, Christian boldness is courageous (i.e., not "a spirit of fear"). Courage is not acting boldly without fear; it is, rather, acting in spite of fear. When Paul said that God hadn't given the Christian a spirit of fear, he didn't mean there is no more fear. He meant, rather, that the debilitating fear that often paralyzes the Christian is not sold in the store of God.

Anyone who lives in our kind of world without fear is a fool. In Mark Twain's cynical small novel titled *The Mysterious Stranger*, the mysterious stranger had told a little boy that a certain man who is anxiety ridden will live his entire life in happiness. Then the man went insane. The little boy was angry and bitter because he felt betrayed. But Satan (the Mysterious Stranger) said:

What an ass you are! Are you so unobservant as not to have found out that sanity and happiness are an impossible combination? No sane man can be happy, for to him life is real, and he sees what a fearful thing it is. Only the mad can be happy, and not many of those. The few that imagine themselves kings or gods are happy, the rest are no happier than the sane. . . . I have taken from this man that trumpery thing which the race regards as a Mind; I have replaced his tin life with a silver-gilt fiction; you see the result—and you criticize! I said I would make him permanently happy, and I have done it. I have made him happy by the only means possible to his race—and you are not satisfied![2]

Too many Christians walk around with the feeling that to be human is a sin. So, we think Christians don't get depressed, or angry, or afraid. That isn't what Paul said. He said that real Christian boldness is courage that comes in the face of real fear. We live in a fallen world where the dangers are very real. What Christ does with the Christian is to give him or her a spirit of courage.

I remember a board meeting I once attended when the whole board was negative on a position about which I was positive. I was the newest member of the board, and to be perfectly honest, I was intimidated by the others (well-known Christian businessmen and national Christian leaders) and had determined, at least in the beginning, to keep my mouth shut. (The principle: Better to be thought a fool than to open one's mouth and remove all doubt.) But I felt so strongly on this particular issue that I felt I ought to say something. So I did.

The problem was once I started, I couldn't stop. Something inside was saying to me, "Shut up, you fool." But I still kept talking. Not only was I talking, but I was talking in unbelievably strong terms. When it was over, I felt like going somewhere and hiding. The motion was tabled, and you could have heard a pin drop. It was one of those embarrassing situations similar to the reaction of an audience to a soloist who can't sing but is doing his or her best.

And then, at the next board meeting, I found that the whole board had changed its mind and reversed itself. The board voted unanimously in favor of my position. Where in the world did I get the courage? I'll tell you where. I got it from God, and once He gave it, I couldn't shut up.

Over and over again in church history, we see ordinary men and women God set on fire. They were as much surprised as anyone else. For instance, Thomas Cranmer was a weak and compromising man. In the sixteenth century, he sided with Henry VIII in the king's efforts to be rid of his wife. While holding some Protestant doctrines, his real allegiance was to the king because he had seen what could happen if one were too strong in one's theological views. He had watched Nicholas Ridley and Hugh Latimer die at the stake, and he knew the same thing could happen to him.

With the fear that can only come when you have faced a horrible reality, he renounced in writing his former views. Then as the time of his own death by fire approached, something happened to this weak man. He stood before the crowd who had gathered to see his execution and cried, "And now I come to the great thing which so much troubleth my conscience, more than any thing that ever I did or said in my whole life, and that is the scattering abroad of writing contrary to the truth [referring to his written renunciation]." Cranmer then renounced his turning from the truth and said, "And forasmuch as my hand hath offended, writing contrary to my heart, therefore this my hand shall first be punished, for when I come to the fire, it shall first be burned."[3]

When he was brought before the stake, he placed his hand, the offending hand with which he had written his renunciation of the truth, in the fire and watched his hand burn before he stepped into the flames himself. Where in the world did this man get that kind of courage? How hard did he have to work to obtain it? He didn't. It was a gift from the Father, who creates bold Christians.

Christian Boldness Is Powerful

Second, Paul said that Christian boldness as opposed to pagan boldness is not only courageous, but also powerful. What was it in

Queen Mary, one of the most powerful monarchs on the face of the earth, that caused her to cringe before John Knox? Knox was only a little man with a very weak and frail body.

Mary, in her frustration with Knox, is said to have cried out to him, "I have borne with you in all your rigorous manner of speaking, both against myself and against my uncles; yea, I have sought your favor by all possible means; I have offered unto you presents and audience whence wherever it pleased you to admonish me, and yet I can not be quit of you. I vow to God I shall be once revenged."

Knox replied, "Madam, I am not master of myself, but must obey Him who commands me to speak plain, and to flatter no flesh upon the face of the earth."[4]

Why did Mary fear the prayers of John Knox more than an army of ten thousand men? Thomas McCrie said, "I know not if ever so much piety and genius were lodged in such a frail and weak body. Certain I am that it will be difficult to find one in whom the gifts of the Holy Spirit shone so bright to the comfort of the church in Scotland."[5]

There is supernatural power in the boldness of the Christian. That power is not always successful, but it is always effective. God takes common men and women and sends them out with a powerful message anointed by a powerful God. Once John Wesley was asked why so many people came to his meetings. He replied, "I set myself on fire, and people come to see me burn." He should have said that God set him on fire.

Christian boldness is an awesome thing to watch. I have seen grown men weep before it; I have seen drug addicts turn from their drugs and alcoholics turn from their bottles because of it; I have seen soldiers cringe in its light; I have seen angry, hostile, abrasive people back away from their plans in the face of it; I have seen sinners repent and saints grow as they are prodded by it. There is something supernaturally powerful about Christian boldness. The problem is that few people have seen that power because not many Christians are willing to exercise it.

During the French Revolution, a speaker in the Legislative Assembly asked, "Why do not our great men, our priests and philosophers, move and save the people?"

A woman in the audience shouted back, "Because they are cast in bronze."

That is the problem. All the boldness in the world is nothing but empty wind. It rails and rants and demands its rights. Nothing ever changes until the terrible people of God stand up. That is when history is changed, lives are changed, and circumstances are changed. The change doesn't come because of the Christian's boldness, but because of God's application of power to the Christian's boldness. That power is one of the ways you can tell the difference between Christian and pagan boldness.

Christian Boldness Is Loving

Third, Paul said that Christian boldness is not only courageous and powerful, but also loving. We are going to have a lot more to say about this in later chapters, but for now let me say that real love is as hard as nails. It is love that refuses to let go until the lover is loved and knows it. A friend of mine said to me once, "Steve, you are a very hard person to love, but, before God, I am determined to love you, and I will."

A few months ago Jerry Falwell was invited by Mark Tanenbaum, International Interreligious Affairs Director for the American Jewish Committee, to address a national gathering of conservative Jewish rabbis at a large hotel on Miami Beach. My friend, Bill Gralnick, the Southeast Regional Director for the AJC, was able to obtain a hard-to-come-by ticket for me. It was an interesting meeting.

Jerry Falwell, who certainly does not represent the views of most rabbis in this country, had come into what appeared to be very hostile territory. Mark Tanenbaum, who has done so much to further understanding between evangelicals and Jews, was not a popular man that evening. As I sat in the audience, trying to look as Jewish as possible, I heard comments of anger expressed about Dr. Tanenbaum for having invited this right-wing, fundamentalist preacher.

It was interesting to watch the body language of the rabbis attending that meeting. The body language reflected a high degree of hostility—arms crossed in anger, raised eyebrows, and angry expressions. But as Falwell began to speak, I noticed a gradual change taking place in the audience. The arms were unfolded, the frowns turned to smiles, and the angry expressions turned to expressions of interest. Soon the rabbis were leaning forward to listen to what Falwell was saying. And the more he talked, the more it became apparent that he was winning a hearing. He did not convert any of the rabbis, of course. He didn't try. But his love for them and what they stood for was so apparent that they were willing to listen. His speech was interrupted several times by applause.

During the question and answer session following his speech, Falwell was asked, "What do you want from us?" Falwell's answer was astounding. He said, "I don't want anything from you. I have everything I need and want. I have come here to tell you that I am going to be your friend, and even if you don't want me to be your friend, I'm still going to be your friend. I have come here to tell you that I love you, and even if you don't want me to love you, I am still going to love you. That is the only reason I came."

Jerry Falwell is not a very popular figure in some circles, but that night I saw a demonstration of Christian boldness characterized by love that I won't soon forget. When I hear the narrow and negative ramblings of Norman Lear about Jerry Falwell, I will remember that night and rejoice in a brother whose bold love was an inspiration.

A Christian is bold, but if that boldness is not characterized by love, the whole point of the boldness is lost. Anybody can be bold, but to be lovingly bold is no small thing. Love remembers the other person. Love looks out for the interests of others. Love sometimes is harsh, strong, and even angry, but it is never destructive.

I once asked my friend Fred Smith, one of the wisest Christians I know, the difference between motivation and manipulation. They often appear to be the same thing. Fred said that while manipulation is for the benefit of the one doing the manipulating, motivation is for the benefit of the motivator *and* the one being motivated. I like that, because it is similar to Christian boldness. Christians don't "win through intimidation." They don't have to! Christian boldness is a boldness that never forgets the other person. You file that kind of boldness under love.

Christian Boldness Has a "Sound Mind"

And then finally, Paul said that Christian boldness, as opposed to pagan boldness, is characterized by a "sound mind." The Greek word Paul uses here for "sound mind" is not an easy word to translate into English. It doesn't mean exactly (as some translations have it) self-control, but rather discipline or perhaps the ability to generate discipline in oneself and in others. It is the ability to control oneself in the face of pressure situations.

That is one of the great differences between Christian boldness and pagan boldness. Pagan boldness is often a simple, visceral reaction to unpleasant circumstances. ("You turkey! Look what you did to my car. If you would watch where you're going, you idiot, it wouldn't happen.") Christian boldness, on the other hand, is planned, directed, and controlled. It is not power without pressure, but power under pressure.

A number of years ago, a good friend of mine by the name of Blair Richardson went home to be with the Lord. That isn't the sad part. The sad part is that he was a young man who had a wonderful wife and a baby on the way.

Blair had been a prize fighter when he found Christ through the ministry of my friend John DeBrine. He had held a number of prize fighting titles and was on his way up. Right after he found Christ, John made him give his testimony often. I used to wonder why John did that because, to be perfectly honest with you, Blair simply couldn't talk. I thought someone ought to give Blair speech lessons.

Blair would sometimes set up a fighting ring down in the slums of Boston to demonstrate his gift of prize fighting. When he got a crowd of young people together, he would tell them about Jesus. By the time Blair died, he had become a very fine communicator with his voice as well as his fists, and he was even teaching speech at one of the colleges in Boston. Blair was used all over the country because he had a tremendous gift with young people.

The church near Boston where I was the pastor had scheduled Blair to speak to the young people. I called him a few weeks before the meeting to confirm that he was coming. I asked him how he was doing, and he said he was fine, but that he had a little headache. "Don't worry, Steve," he said, "I'm going to be there, and we are going to see God do a great thing." That night, however, he was rushed to the hospital and before the dawn was dead from a brain tumor.

John DeBrine talked to Blair's wife, Beverly, shortly after Blair's death. He told her, "Beverly, up to this point when you have talked about your relationship to Christ, people have listened, but most people have said, 'Sure, she's a Christian. She has everything going for her. A husband who looks like a Greek god, a baby on the way, a wonderful life. If I had all that, I would be a Christian too.' But, Beverly, those same people are still watching, and they want to know if your faith works in the hard places. They will hear what you say now a lot more than they heard before, so be careful."

Of course our young people were devastated that Blair had died, but we decided to have the youth banquet anyway. And while Beverly Richardson couldn't come, she did write a letter to be read at the banquet. Let me quote from that letter:

Dear Young People,

   Since I am unable to be with you at your banquet, I wanted to send along greetings to you by letter.

As you can well imagine these are difficult days, but I want you to know that my Saviour, Jesus Christ, knows and understands. He has surrounded me with His love and given real peace in my heart.

The wonderful thing about the sorrow I feel over my personal loss of Blair is that it is a sorrow with hope! Blair is with our Lord in heaven and far happier now than even when we were together—and we were very happy.

Why do I know where Blair is right now? Is it because Blair was a good man? No. Is it because he tried to help young people? No. Well, then is it because he always went to church? No. Blair is in heaven today because he was a sinner saved by what Jesus Christ did for him on Calvary's cross. When Blair was twenty-one, he came humbly to the Saviour and confessed that he indeed was a sinner and asked Jesus to come with forgiveness and live through his life. On March 5th Blair saw the Lord face to face.

Young people, I know that Blair certainly did not expect to leave us that day, but he was ready. He had no opportunity for a last minute decision for Christ.

Tonight I would ask those of you who have not accepted Jesus Christ to take a good look at your life. What is it that would hold you back? The things of this world satisfy for only a brief time, but our Saviour gives true meaning to life here on earth and then eternal life with Him. Is anything here worth keeping us from that?

For those of us who are Christians, I would ask that we really recommit our lives to the Lord so that He can really use us. There are so many who do not know Christ. Won't you let Him use you to lead others to Him in the days ahead?

You will be in my thoughts and prayers tonight. Let this be the most important night of your lives!

With Love in Christ,
Beverly Richardson

That letter is the best definition I know of for what Paul said characterizes Christian boldness. I can see someone writing a letter like that a couple of years after the death of one they loved. But to write that kind of letter less than two weeks after her husband had died is nothing less than a demonstration of self-control and a sound mind.

Kent Keller, the minister to young people at the church I serve, gave me a "tongue in cheek" advertisement for a new plan to make youth groups come alive. I think it is from the *Wittenberg Door*, and it is an advertisement for Y.I.T. (Youth Intimidation Training). The ad says that this new method will radically change youth ministries all over the country. It reads: "The scene is set. You're sharing the plan of salvation with a youth. He doesn't buy it. You've been patient and persuasive but he's obstinate. So you ask him if he'd like to step outside. There you beat the fool out of him. Dynamic? All over America Youth Directors are turning to Y.I.T. . . . The youth of the eighties are a belligerent lot."

That, ladies and gentlemen, is the danger. Christian boldness is sometimes similar to pagan boldness, but pagan boldness is a counterfeit. Frank Sinatra sang, "I did it my way." Christians must sing, "I did it the Father's way." Christian boldness is always for the Father, and that makes all the difference in the world.

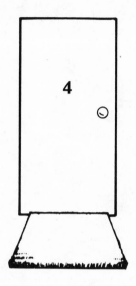

"Whoever is fearful and afraid, let him turn and depart at once from Mount Gilead."

JUDGES 7:3b

The Danger
in
Deviation

4

A very wise and bold man once said:

> I do not choose to be a common man. It is my right to be uncommon—if I can. I seek opportunity—not security. I do not wish to be a kept citizen, humbled and dulled by having the state look after me. I want to take the calculated risk; to dream and to build; to fail and to succeed. I refuse to barter incentive for a dole. I prefer the challenges of life to the guaranteed existence; the thrill of fulfillment to the stale calm of utopia. I will not trade freedom for beneficence nor my dignity for a handout. I will never cower before any master nor bend to any threat. It is my heritage to stand erect, proud and unafraid; to think and act for myself; enjoy the benefits of my creations; and to face the world boldly and say, "This I have done." All this is what it means to be free.[1]

That statement refers, of course, to the great power and freedom to be found in democratic capitalism. It is the kind of quotation that causes most of us to feel better about a system of government where we can hold our heads up and speak our minds. It is the kind of system where one can enjoy the benefits of success and accept the responsibilities of failure. It is a call to freedom, responsibility, and integrity.

But the fact is, when you get right down to it, most people are not as interested in freedom as they are in security. Given the clear option between freedom (with its attendant responsibility and problems) and dictatorship (with its attendant structure and limits), most people will pick dictatorship every time. Why? Because we want to be secure and safe, not free and responsible.

Dr. Ronald Berman, professor of Renaissance Literature at the University of California, in a symposium on freedom sponsored by the Rockford Institute, made a very telling statement:

> According to the politics of mental health, the social and political conditions we live under cause neurosis. Neurosis is to be known by unhappiness. Unhappiness reflects directly on that political freedom under which it transpires. Political freedom is therefore in opposition to personal freedom. This last accounts for several mysteries of cultural politics. The first such mystery concerns our extraordinary hospitality toward totalitarian idealism. As has been widely noted, pilgrims from the West give their most enthusiastic and unqualified praise to the spirit of Soviet or Chinese society. They do this while readily admitting that actual daily life is repressive. But they admire the tranquilized character of those under communist rule, especially their freedom from doubt. This is less naive than is generally thought. The pilgrims know about censorship and the one-party state and the secret police. But they prefer them, at least for other people, to the political ambiguities of freedom. A decade ago Norman Mailer found that Cubans were happy—or that he was happy at the thought of happy Cubans. Today the same applies to the sympathetic visitor of Vietnam or the Soviet Union. It is not that such visitors are unaware of tyranny, but that they believe there are more important things than freedom for mental health.[2]

The point is this: Freedom sounds good until you get right down to what it costs, and when that happens most people will opt for something less than freedom.

DO WE REALLY WANT TO BE BOLD?

So far we have been talking politically, but it is just as true in religion as it is in politics. Most of us would rather have someone else tell us what God says than to listen to God speaking; most of us would rather read a commentary than the Bible; most of us would rather be in submission to a religious authority figure than to take responsibility ourselves; most of us would rather listen to a sermon than preach one. Someone has said that many Christians are running around with an umbilical cord looking for a place to plug it in.

And so, it seems to me, it is important before we go any further in our pursuit of Christian boldness that we decide whether we *want* Christian boldness. I heard about a speaker who was addressing a conference of Christian athletes who said, "You think I have come here to make you feel better. That isn't true. I have come here to bind up the wounds from the last battle before I send you out to the next one."

Someone tells the story of a college football team that was losing an important game by a wide margin. The coach stood on the side-lines yelling to his team, "Give the ball to Jack! Give the ball to Jack!" But Jack never got the ball, and the team continued to lose. The coach yelled again, "Give the ball to Jack!"

One of the players finally yelled back to the coach, "Jack says he doesn't want the ball!"

As you read through this book, you may simply not want the ball. Better to decide that now than later, because there is no one more miserable than the person who is reaching for someone else's goal.

I spend a portion of my time teaching seminary students, and one of the pastoral traits that I urge my students to develop is a "mean streak." One of the problems in many American churches is that pastors have become "free bait" for neurotic (and they are a small minority) church members. If the members don't like the way a pastor parts his hair or ties his tie, they feel free to tell him. If they don't like his wife's dress, they tell him. If they don't like the way he smiles, they tell him. I could write a book on the comments people make to a pastor, comments they would never think of making to anybody else.

Not too long ago I was talking to a pastor who was in some serious trouble with his congregation. He was being criticized and made fun of in a shameful way. As we talked, it became apparent to me that it was necessary for this young man to develop a "mean streak" or he wasn't going to survive. He told me that he felt he had been called to "love" his people and to understand them even when they were cruel and abusive. I said to him that while I felt he should be loving and kind, it was very important that he be honest and strong too. I suggested that he bring the people who had been making the comments before the ruling body of the church and call them either to refrain from such comments in the future or to justify their disturbance of the peace and unity of the church.

That young pastor made a very interesting comment to me. He said, "Steve, I know that is what I should do, but I'm just not made that way. I feel my ministry is to pour oil on troubled waters, not put a match to it." Needless to say, that young man is no longer in the ministry. He didn't have enough oil for all the troubled waters. He is now selling insurance.

THE PRICE OF BOLDNESS

When the Christian gets serious about Christian boldness, there is a price to pay. What Jesus said about discipleship needs to be said about boldness: "For which of you, intending to build a tower, does not sit down first and count the cost, whether he has enough to finish it—lest, after he has laid the foundation, and is not able to finish it, all who see it begin to mock him, saying, 'This man began to build and was not able to finish'" (Luke 14:28–30).

The question this passage raises is this: If I decide to go the way of boldness, what is it going to cost me? Let's talk about the price tag.

Risk Sometimes Ends in Failure

First, Christian boldness presupposes that you will sometimes fail because you are required to risk. The easiest way I know to avoid failure is never to risk. In my pagan days I played a lot of poker. As a matter of fact, you can learn a lot about life and people from playing poker. Kenny Rogers wasn't the only one to discover that. When you play poker and you are never willing to risk, you must face the prospect that you will never win. Most people who play poker and never risk may be down a little one week and up a little the next week, but they will never have the satisfaction of taking a large "pot." Life is like that. If you never risk saying something inappropriate, if you never risk a relationship by telling the truth, if you never risk the acceptance of your friends by being faithful to Christ, then you will be safe; but you will never know the excitement and the great rewards of risk.

There is a popular minister in this country who is often the brunt of jokes and criticism. He continues to succeed, and the more he succeeds the more he is criticized. A friend of mine wrote him a note recently after a very critical article had appeared in a prominent magazine. My friend wrote, "If you are tired of the criticism, there is a very easy way to bring it to a stop. Simply fail."

Well, that is not entirely accurate. As a matter of fact, if he should have significant failure, the criticism would not stop. However, if he had never tried to succeed, he would never have been criticized.

One of the important points I try to make with seminary students is that if they are in doubt about saying something in the pulpit, they ought to say it. When I say that, there are often questions from the students. They wonder if that isn't a bit radical; they wonder if maybe that kind of thing could lead to saying something improper in the pulpit; they think a lot of people will get upset. I always say, "Yes, all of that is true. However, if you risk, the people who sit under your ministry will never sleep, and you will find that much of the time it was in the area of risk that you communicated truth in a way the people could hear and understand."

Martin Luther said that if we sin we ought to "sin boldly." What did he mean by that? He meant that there is nothing worse than a Christian who cowers over in a corner, whining about the perils of the pagan world. For God's sake, I think Luther would say, "Quit whining and do something—even if it is done badly."

71

I live in a large city, and when you live in a city you begin to think a lot about safety. You can put bars on your windows, spotlights in your yard, and bolts on your doors. You can buy a big dog, a big gun, and a big fence. You can set up a security system that no one could break, and "Keep Out, Bad Dog" signs that no one but a fool would ignore. You can refuse to go for a walk or risk speaking to a stranger. You can have police patrolling the neighborhood and neighbors you are afraid to know. You can do all of that, but the problem is that once you have done it all you are no different from the man who is in a solitary confinement cell. He is usually safe too, but his freedom is gone.

In the twenty-fifth chapter of Matthew Jesus talked about a man who refused to risk. Jesus said that before a certain master went away on a journey, he called his servants and gave them his goods. He gave one man five talents, another two, and another one. When he returned from his journey, he called his servants to give an account. The servant who had received the five talents had made five talents more, and the servant who had been given two talents also doubled his amount. But the man who had received the one talent said, "Lord, I knew you to be a hard man, reaping where you have not sown, and gathering where you have not scattered seed. And I was afraid, and went and hid your talent in the ground. Look, there you have what is yours" (vv. 24–25).

Do you remember what the master said to that man? He said, "You wicked and lazy servant, you knew that I reap where I have not sown, and gather where I have not scattered seed. Therefore you ought to have deposited my money with the bankers, and at my coming I would have received back my own with interest. Therefore take the talent from him, and give it to him who has ten talents" (vv. 26–28).

One of the things I have noticed about a lot of Christians is that they are afraid to risk checking out their faith against the arguments of unbelievers. They operate on the general principle that their faith may not be much, but it's all they've got. If they challenge a pagan, the pagan may rob them of the little they have, so they just remain quiet.

At the church I serve, we sometimes have what we call "Skeptics' Forum." We invite atheists and agnostics to come and meet with the pastor (me) to find some honest answers to their honest questions. We promise that no one will beat them over the head with a Bible or pray over them (at least in their presence). I am the only Christian who is allowed in the room, and the meeting is usually held in my study. The skeptics set the format by listing the subjects they would like to discuss, and each evening I will talk for about ten minutes on the particular subject. Then, for the next two hours, the skeptics are given a chance to go after me.

The first Skeptics' Forum was extremely frightening for me. I thought these unbelievers had a deep, thoughtful commitment to their unbelief. As a matter of fact, just the opposite was true. Most skeptics' intellectual acumen is about as shallow as a child's wading pool. The hardest thing about Skeptics' Forum was to refrain from saying, "That is the dumbest thing I have ever heard. I can't believe you would say something as stupid as that!" Of course, I never said anything like that, but I was reminded of Billy Sunday's comment that "a sinner can repent, but stupid is forever."

From the forum I learned it was only in risking that I discovered the truth of my faith. If I had never risked, I probably would have held on to the little faith that I professed, but I would have always wondered if it were true. Its truth was discovered in risk.

If you want to exercise bold Christianity, you have to be prepared to face the possibility of failure, because you have to risk. Too many Christians refuse to risk politically, socially, or spiritually. They have traded a prison called security for the excitement of standing on the "firing line."

Some People Won't Like You

Second, if you decide to be a bold Christian, you have to face the reality that not everyone is going to like you. Most of us have a great need to be loved, and because of that need many of us sell our souls.

We commit some of our worst and most sinful acts simply because we want to be loved.

Amma Sarah, one of the desert Christians of the fourth and fifth centuries, said, "If I prayed God that all men should approve of my conduct, I should find myself a penitent at the door of each one, but I shall rather pray that my heart may be pure towards all."[3]

One of the hardest lessons I ever learned was that I can't please everyone. I want to; I want to be what everyone wants me to be; I want everyone to love me. The problem is that it simply can't be done; and a pastor who doesn't understand that will never be effective. The problem isn't just for clergy, however; it is the problem with a lot of Christians. We believe spurious doctrines, refuse to ask questions, are afraid to confront, stifle protests, keep quiet when we ought to speak, allow ourselves to be manipulated—all because we are afraid that people won't love us if we don't please them.

C. S. Lewis, in a very insightful essay entitled "The Inner Ring," has written:

> I believe that in all men's lives at certain periods, and in many men's lives at all periods between infancy and extreme old age, one of the most dominant elements is the desire to be inside the local Ring and the terror of being left outside. . . . Of all passions the passion for the Inner Ring is most skillful in making a man who is not yet a very bad man do very bad things.[4]

There is a crisis in this country among pastors who have a need to be liked. I can understand that because it is one of my problems too. Have you ever noticed the Christian liturgy that takes place, not during the worship service, but after it? The pastor goes to the front door of the church, and everyone files past him. As they pass him the liturgy requires that they say, "Pastor, that was a wonderful sermon." The liturgy then requires that the pastor respond by saying, "Thank you for saying that. I'm pleased that God used it."

Now, I suspect this practice is fine except when the pastor has preached a "bomb." He knows it and the congregation knows it too.

During the sermon people were checking their watches, and then they were shaking them to make sure they weren't broken. Everybody was bored, and the sermon died before it got to the first pew. Never mind—the Christian liturgy is chiseled in concrete; the pastor still has to go to the front door, and the people still have to file past him with the same comment and the same response.

If you are not a pastor, you won't understand how terrible those times are. The problem comes, however, when a pastor wants, more than anything in the world, to avoid those kinds of days. He begins to write his sermons to please his congregation. He knows there is truth that needs to be said, but he doesn't say it because it might offend someone. He knows he needs to be strong, but if he is too strong people might be upset, so he passes out pious pablum that doesn't offend anyone.

Because a pastor's self-identity is so caught up in what he does in the pulpit, it isn't a long distance between being kind, sweet, and insipid in the pulpit and being kind, sweet, and insipid in every area of his life.

I once read a book with a great title: *Bible in Pocket, Gun in Hand*. It was about the frontier preachers in America and their determination to preach the gospel whether or not anybody wanted to listen. They would have been very uncomfortable in many contemporary churches. In fact, most of our churches would have been uncomfortable with them. They simply would not have been able to play the game.

But, lest you think I am just talking about a clergy problem, let me say that the average Christian wants to be loved too. That desire causes more Christians to keep quiet at inappropriate times than anything I know.

During the "Jesus Movement" of the sixties and early seventies, I was the pastor of a Presbyterian church near Boston. We were the big Presbyterian church up on the hill, and if nothing else, we were certainly proper. And then Jesus began sending some rather smelly, unkempt, vocal young Christians into our fellowship. I must say that the dear people in that church, its pastor included, did quite well in accepting those kids. But, to be perfectly honest with you, it wasn't easy.

I remember one time when they decided to have a "Jesus March" around the church before the Sunday morning worship service. They made "Jesus" signs, printed up "Jesus" tee shirts, and carried "Jesus" banners. They got all the kids in the Sunday school to march with them. Now that was rather difficult for Presbyterians to absorb by itself; but when they started the "Jesus" yell, it almost brought the whole thing to an end. (It went, "Give me a 'J,' give me an 'E,' give me an 'S,'" and so on.) You could hear the yell all over the neighborhood. I thought, *What will people think? What will the elderly people coming to church during the march think? What do I think?*

Occasionally during the Sunday evening service, I would ask a few of those young people to stand before the congregation and tell what Christ had done for them. You should have heard some of those little speeches. They talked about their rebellion, their drugs, their guilt, and how Jesus had changed everything. The problem was that their language was rather graphic. To be perfectly honest with you, graphic language has no place in a Presbyterian church, but I let them continue because what they were saying was so real. There were times when I hid in the chair behind the big column to the right of the pulpit and prayed nervously, "Lord, help him/her to say it in a way that is a little softer." But they never did.

During those days, and they were exciting, I discovered what made those "Jesus people" so winsome. They cared more for what Jesus thought than for what anybody else thought. That was a good lesson for me and the congregation.

If you are going to be bold, you have to face the fact that a lot of people won't understand. If you are going to be different, you must realize before you decide to be different that most people want you to be like them, and if you aren't they won't like it. Count that cost before you decide to be different.

You Might Lose Your Peace

And then there is another cost that must be paid if you decide to become a bold Christian: It will sometimes rob you of your peace. "Wait," you say, "I thought that Jesus gave peace in the midst of turmoil. The least I could expect is personal peace in the conflict." Yes, that is true, but you need to know the kind of peace about which Jesus spoke.

First, let me give you a principle. The peace this side of conflict is not worth a hill of beans. In fact, it is not the kind of peace about which Jesus spoke. The peace this side of conflict is not biblical peace at all; it is simply apathetic contentment. If you want to be contented like a cow, drink lots of milk and keep your mouth shut. Only dead people and cows know that kind of peace.

In contrast, whereas the peace on this side of conflict is not worth a bag of chicken feed, the peace on the other side of conflict is worth anything it costs you.

Have you ever heard those Christians who say they know God's will because they "feel peace" about it? I don't want to say that isn't the way to know God's will, but let me tell you about my experience. I have never felt peace about anything that was God's will. In fact, the place of my greatest turmoil and conflict has often come when I was in God's will.

I want you to go with me to the garden of Gethsemane, where a Man by the name of Jesus was about to die. He knew He was going to die, and He knew that the death He faced was going to be horrible.

When a man is frightened, he wants someone with him. Jesus was God, but He was also a man, and He asked His disciples to stay with Him as He prayed. Matthew told the story:

> Then Jesus came with them to a place called Gethsemane, and said to the disciples, "Sit here while I go and pray over there." And He took with Him Peter and the two sons of Zebedee, and He began to be sorrowful and deeply distressed. Then He said to them, "My soul is exceedingly sorrowful, even to death. Stay here and watch with Me." He went a little farther and fell on His face, and prayed, saying "O My Father, if it is possible, let this cup pass from Me; nevertheless, not as I will, but as You will" (Matt. 26:36–39).

The physician Luke with his practiced medical eye said, "And being in agony, He prayed more earnestly. And His sweat became like great drops of blood falling down to the ground" (Luke 22:44).

Now, if you think Jesus felt peace in that garden as He prepared to face the cross, I have some land to sell you in the middle of a swamp in Florida. He was not peaceful, and if Jesus was not peaceful when He was in the center of the will of God, why in the world do we think we should feel peaceful when we are in the center of the will of God?

But on the other side of the conflict we see a peace that is nothing less than supernatural. When Jesus was dying, He prayed for those who killed Him to be forgiven, and His final words were, "Father, into Your hands I commend My spirit" (Luke 23:46).

If you decide to be different, to stand, to risk, the resultant "feeling" might well be, "I wish I had kept my mouth shut. How could I have been so stupid?" But as time passes, there will be a peace that you have never known, a peace that says, "I didn't like what I did. It made me feel out of sorts and anxious. But I did what God said." At night, in those few minutes just before sleep, you will be able to "rest easy" and "sleep clean" with the peace of one who has been faithful.

In this book I want to talk to you about how to be a bold Christian. I'm not going to promise you success, acceptance, and peace. You have to pay a price for anything of value. However, I do promise that ultimate success will be yours, that the Father will accept you even if no one else does, and that when it comes your time to die, you will be able to say, "Father, I did what You told me to do."

Someone tells the story of the missionary who came back to America after an extended mission tour. He was Christ's faithful servant, and it was good to get home. It happened that he was on the same ship that was bringing Theodore Roosevelt back to New York from an overseas trip. There was a great crowd at the dock, and at first the missionary thought they had come to welcome him. But soon it became apparent that they had gathered for Roosevelt.

As Roosevelt walked off the ship onto the dock, the band started playing and people started shouting. The crowd lifted Roosevelt on their shoulders and marched off down the street.

The missionary then made his way to the dock. He was alone. He had tears in his eyes, and he prayed, "Father, I have been serving You all these years. I've been faithful. I have proclaimed Your message. But when this man comes home, he has a band and a crowd. When I come home, there is no one to meet me, no one to shout, no one to make me feel welcome."

It was then that the missionary heard the voice. It was a voice he knew intimately. It was the voice of the God he served. He heard the words he would remember until the day he died.

"Son, you aren't home yet."

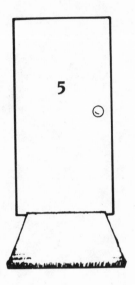

"But let your 'Yes' be 'Yes,' and your 'No,' 'No.' For whatever is more than these is from the evil one."

MATTHEW 5:37

"No" Is Not a Dirty Word

5

Thomas Kelly, in A *Testament of Devotion*, spoke of God's special concern for all His creation. He then pointed out to believers the necessity of using God as a model of concern while at the same time realizing that a believer's limitations force him or her to "specialize" the concern:

But it is a particularization of my responsibility in a world too vast and a lifetime too short for me to carry all responsibilities. My cosmic love, or the Divine Lover loving within me, cannot accomplish its full intent, which is universal saviorhood, within the limits of three score years and ten. But the Loving Presence does not burden us equally with all things, but considerately puts upon each of us just a few central tasks, as emphatic responsibilities. For each of us these special undertakings are our share in the joyous burdens of love.

Thus the state of having a concern has a foreground and a background. In the foreground is the special task, uniquely illuminated, toward which we feel a special yearning and care....But in the background is a second level, or layer, of universal concern for all the multitude of good things that need doing. Toward them all we feel kindly, but we are dismissed from active service in most of them. And we have an easy mind in the presence of desperately real needs which are not our direct responsibility. We cannot die on every cross, nor are we expected to.[1]

Spurgeon was fond of telling his students, "Learn to say no. It will do you more good than Latin." He was right, but as a matter of fact, most Christians simply don't know how to say no to anything that sounds religious or which carries the adjective of "Christian."

We understand that a Christian is to say no to practices that are "no-nos" in the Bible. We are called to say no to temptation; we are not to be engaged in sexual immorality, drunkenness, and lying. Christians are to say no to the devil, to false gods, and to false men. The Ten Commandments give us a number of "thou shalt nots," and we are very clear on them.

The problem with most Christians is not that they don't know how to say no (though we often don't) to bad things. The problem is that we haven't learned to say no to good things when we should.

I do a substantial amount of travel in my speaking and have noticed in nearly every place I have gone that most committed Christians are tired. They are tired because they operate out of the spurious notion that Christians are supposed to do everything that anybody tells them to do if it is Christian.

I have a dear pastor friend who has many talents, but one of his best talents is taking up an offering. He used to conduct large youth rallies, and every time I attended those rallies, I decided before I went what I was going to put in the offering, because I knew that if I waited until I got there I would end up giving everything I had in my pockets.

My friend would often say before the offering, "Look around you. The odds are that you are sitting next to a nonbeliever, and that non-believer is watching you. In our country you can tell what a person believes by looking at his checkbook. What is that nonbeliever going to think if you only put a dollar in the offering plate? I'll tell you what he is going to think; he is going to think that you don't really believe it, or that you only believe it a dollar's worth." At other times he would say, "If you had gone to a movie tonight it would have cost you five dollars, and you add to that the dinner and the gas money and you are up to twenty-five dollars. Do you love Jesus as much as a movie, dinner, and car fare?"

By the time he finished his announcement before the offering, I had opened my billfold, taken everything out, and dug into my pocket for all my loose change too. I want you to know that I simply could not let Jesus down in my witness to the pagan next to whom I was sitting, and I certainly loved Jesus more than a movie!

One time my friend was away on vacation and asked me to conduct the rally. I tried some of his "techniques" when the offering time came up, and I thought I had done quite well. After the rally I went to the back room where the offering was being counted and found myself rather proud of the fact that there had been a good offering. I commented to the secretary who was overseeing the counting that I felt we had done well. She smiled and said, "Yes, it isn't bad, but Jack (not his name) would have gotten twice as much."

THE THREE LIES THAT LEAD TO YES

The offering taken by my friend is a good analogy of how Christians get manipulated into saying yes when we ought to say no. Let's analyze some of the reasons why we say yes at the wrong times. It is usually because we have believed three lies.

Believing God Always Wants a Yes

First we say yes when we ought to say no because we genuinely believe God always wants us to say yes. There is a great lesson to learn in John's account of Jesus' raising of His friend Lazarus from the dead. You will find the account in the eleventh chapter of the Gospel of John.

> Now a certain man was sick, Lazarus of Bethany, the town of Mary and her sister Martha. It was that Mary who anointed the Lord with fragrant oil and wiped His feet with her hair, whose brother Lazarus was sick. Therefore the sisters sent to him, saying, "Lord, behold, he whom You love is sick." When

Jesus heard that, He said, "This sickness is not unto death, but for the glory of God, that the Son of God may be glorified through it." Now Jesus loved Martha and her sister and Lazarus. So, when He heard that he was sick, *He stayed two more days in the place where He was* (vv. 1–6, italics mine).

When Jesus finally got to Bethany, Lazarus was dead. Martha, the sister of Lazarus, gave Jesus a reprimand: "Then Martha, as soon as she heard that Jesus was coming, went and met Him, but Mary was sitting in the house. Then Martha said to Jesus, 'Lord, if You had been here, my brother would not have died'" (vv. 20–21). Later Mary, from whom you would have expected more because she understood Jesus better, was just as upset as Martha. "Then, when Mary came where Jesus was, and saw Him, she fell down at His feet, saying to Him, 'Lord, if You had been here, my brother would not have died'" (v. 32).

The interesting thing about that whole episode is that Jesus was in tune with God's agenda, and He didn't care about everybody else's agenda. If we had been there, we would have said to Him, "Jesus, don't You care about Your friend? He's sick and You can help, and all You do is sit here." If we had been there, we would have told Him that His "Christian duty" demanded that He do something. We would have told Him that no Christian ever turns away from any need. How can you say no, we would ask, to such a great need? And if we had said that, we would have been absolutely wrong.

Let me give you an important principle: Immediate need is *not* God's call for immediate action. God's call for immediate action is the *only* call for immediate action.

One of my dear friends is Cleve Bell, the director of Riverside House, a ministry that deals with people while they are in prison and also works with them after they're released. Every time I'm around Cleve, I feel guilty that I'm not doing more in prison work. After all, Jesus said (Matthew 25) we ought to visit the prisoners. Sometimes I get so guilty that I go with Cleve to one of our jails. (I have a similar feeling when I'm around Chuck Colson. I sometimes go with him too.)

One day Jim Green (one of the most effective youth workers in the country), Eddie Waxer (who has a great international sports ministry), Cleve Bell, and I had lunch together. Cleve was telling us about what God was doing in the prisons. Then, because he had another appointment, Cleve had to leave lunch early. I said to Jim and Eddie after Cleve had left, "Don't you guys sometimes feel that we ought to be doing more of what Cleve is doing? His commitment to those prisoners puts me to shame."

Jim and Eddie were on me like "ugly on an ape." Eddie said, "Steve, have you ever had any indication that God has called you to prison work?" I allowed that I didn't, and then Eddie said, "Steve, if you aren't called to that work, stay away from it. All you will do is fail to do what God called you to do, and mess up what He didn't call you to do."

Jim said, "Steve, I pray for Cleve and support his work, but God gave me a burden for kids. I'm going to do what God told me to do." They were right, and I was wrong.

In Calvin Miller's first volume of his delightful Singer trilogy, the Singer (Jesus) had encountered a miller who was filled with pity because of his great pain and deformity. His arm and hand were scarred and had become practically useless because of an accident. The Singer offered to help, and the miller replied, "It cannot be so easy, Singer. Would you wave your magic wand above such suffering and have it all be done with? . . . Stop your mocking. I am a sick old man whom life has cheated of a hand. The nightly pain has already now begun. The Season of my hope is gone."

And then the miller fell on the floor and moaned in a great spasm of pain. Miller wrote, "His surging pain caused him to cry, 'O God deliver me from this body. . . . I never can be well and whole as other men.' He waited for the Singer to join him in his pity, but when he raised his head for understanding, the door stood open on the night and the Singer was nowhere to be seen."[2]

Just like the Singer, we will come to places where we simply have to turn away. These are places to which God has not called us either because the situation doesn't fit into His plan or because the circumstances do not call for our involvement. The Singer could not help the miller because the miller's self-pity required anyone who would help, including the Singer, to participate in his pity. That was not on the Singer's agenda.

The point is this: Find out what God has told you to do, and then say no to the rest. One of Satan's greatest tricks is to get us off God's track. There are a multitude of reasons why God would have us do one thing and not another (e.g., He is teaching a lesson, He has someone else chosen to do the job, He is working out a greater good, and so on). You see, God is the great chess Master, and He is the only one who sees the whole board. We are to play the part the chess Master would have us play and trust that He knows what He is doing.

Let me take an aside here and say a word about how a believer can know what it is God wants him or her to do. There are a number of good books on the subject of determining God's will, and I don't want to take time for a detailed analysis of the subject. However, I have four principles I follow in that determination. First, I look at Scripture. The Bible is the only absolute guide to what ought to be the direction of my life (see 2 Tim. 3:16–17).

Second, there are circumstances. Ecclesiastes 9:10 says, "Whatever your hand finds to do, do it with your might." I believe that where I am is where I'm supposed to be, and what I am doing is what I am supposed to be doing unless God, who is perfectly capable of letting me know, tells me otherwise.

Third, there are the spiritual gifts God has given. It is clear that God has not called me to sing, given the fact that I sound like a fog horn (see 1 Cor. 12:4–31 and Eph. 4:1–16).

Finally, there are my brothers and sisters in Christ who love me enough to tell me the truth. Others usually are able to see my gifts better than I can, and I am always open to their input concerning the direction of my life (see Eph. 5:21).

Believing No Will Hurt Our Witness

The second reason we say yes when we ought to say no is that we are afraid of what people will think. There is probably nothing in this world that will kill a Christian faster than constantly being on-stage before the world, playing to an audience who will determine whether we are good, pure, or faithful.

Thomas Kelly emphasized this point in his work A *Testament of Devotion*:

> But there is something about deepest humility which makes men bold. For utter obedience is self-forgetful obedience. No longer do we hesitate and shuffle and apologize because, say we, we are weak, lowly creatures and the world is a pack of snarling wolves among whom we are sent as sheep by the Shepherd. . . . If we live in complete humility in God, we can smile in patient assurance as we work. Will you be wise enough and humble enough to be little fools of God? For who can finally stay His power?[3]

There is probably nothing worse than a constant "acting out" of what we think of as a witness to the world. As a matter of fact, we are witnesses to what Christ has made of us, and not to what we pretend to be. When we get those confused, we become true hypocrites.

Have you ever heard pagans refer to Christians as hypocrites because Christians are not good? I hear it all the time, and I realize how miserably we have failed in communicating what the gospel of Jesus Christ is all about. A hypocrite is one who proclaims with his or her words or life what he or she doesn't believe. When a pagan says, "Those Christians are hypocrites because they pray on their knees on Sunday and prey on their neighbors the rest of the week," they simply haven't understood the gospel. If I should say that the Christian faith is for good people, call myself a Christian, and then am not good, I am indeed a hypocrite. However, that isn't what the Bible teaches at all. The Bible teaches that Christ came to save sinners—not good people. Therefore, my witness is not to my purity, kindness, and love—it is to Christ's purity, His kindness, and His love.

If your witness consists of your purity, those who know you will legitimately call you a hypocrite, and those who don't will think that the Christian faith is only for good people. All you will see of them is their "heels and elbows" as they run in the opposite direction.

Is goodness a witness? Of course it is, but only the goodness that Christ gives the Christian; and when He gives it, it is never arrogant and judgmental. Is absolute goodness a witness? Impossible! "No one is good but One, that is, God" (Matt. 19:17). If our sin can't be used as a witness as well as our goodness, we have a serious problem.

I have a friend who recently became a Christian. She failed miserably in her sexual relationship with a young man who saw nothing wrong with having sex with anyone who was willing. "After all," he said, "it is just a normal need like eating and exercise. How could it be wrong?" My friend fell for that type of idiocy and then came to my study sobbing her heart out. I listened to her confession, and then I reminded her of the reason Christ died for her.

Next I said to her, "Joan, you have a great opportunity to witness to this man. Why don't you go to him and ask his forgiveness for having betrayed the most important person in your life, Jesus?"

She did it, and he didn't know how to handle it.

She went to this man and said, "I want to ask your forgiveness. Sex is a beautiful thing, and I can't say that I don't enjoy sex, but last night I did something far worse than sleep with you. I failed to be faithful to Christ who loves me. I gave lie to the central belief of my life. I'm forgiven and things are okay between Christ and me, but where I really failed was in not showing you clearly about Christ. When I slept with you last night, my greatest sin was in hiding Christ. Will you forgive me?"

Now, that man is not a Christian because of her witness, but he is thinking about it. She had become one beggar telling another beggar where she found bread, and that was a whole lot different from one actor telling another actor where he can do some more acting.

What people think about God is not dependent on you or me. If you get to thinking that, the God you worship is not the God of the Bible. He is an idol you created who is weak and helpless without our efforts to help Him along. The God of the universe will be praised and honored because this whole thing is His show and not ours. So forget about the act. The world and God can do without it.

Philip Yancey, in his good book *Open Windows*, wrote about how people are moved by hearing great music. He noted that God is often communicated in great music even if the musician is not so great.

> Perhaps crusty old Beethoven, who, it is said, angrily shook a fist at the thundering heavens before relaxing into death, meant the words as he rolled them over and over in his mind, searching out the most profound way of communicating them. The music, so powerful a carrier of thoughts too unearthly to be fully expressed, assumes its own power, possessing composer, conductor, performers, audience.

And then Yancey, speaking of the eternal in music, commented:

> I am not alone—even hardened music critics are vulnerable. Reviewing the Chicago Symphony's recent recording of Brahms' *German Requiem*, Heuwell Tircuit of the *San Francisco Chronicle* wrote, "The performance is divine (in several senses). It constitutes an overpowering experience, one which is not only technically and stylistically perfect, but moving in an uncanny religious way. When the chorus sings of *The Living Christ*, even an atheist can believe in Him."[4]

Listen, if you are a believer, God has given you a song. Don't be so concerned with anything but the song. It is the song that will draw people to Christ, not you. So, just sing the song.

To be perfectly honest with one another, we are not so afraid of what the world will think about our God as we are about what other Christians will think of us. That, by the way, is what "cultural Christianity" is all about. We take what the Bible says about being a Christian, overlay it with what we "mature" Christians think about being a Christian, then we go and try to force other Christians into the mold we created. May God forgive us!

One time as I participated in a Wednesday evening prayer meeting at the church I serve, one of the "mature" Christians gave testimony to what Christ had done in his life. He talked about being delivered by God's Spirit from a number of sins. The next day I had lunch with another man (a new Christian) who had attended that prayer meeting. After the chit-chat was over, he said to me, "Pastor, I've decided to leave the church." I asked him why, and he told me that he was never going to make it. He said, "Pastor, I listened to Bill last night, and I just don't have what he has."

I am bound by the secrets people tell me, so I couldn't reveal what I knew about the man who had given his testimony. But I said to my new Christian friend, "Listen, the first thing you have to learn about the Christian life is not to take too seriously what some other Christians say in testimony meetings. You say you don't have what he has. Well, he doesn't have what he says he has, and if he were a little bit more honest, you could get about the business of the Christian life without trying to be something you're not."

Isn't it terrible that I have to tell a new Christian he shouldn't take too seriously what people say in testimony meetings? But you and I both know it's true. The church ought to be a fellowship of people who are terribly honest. The reason we aren't honest is that we are playing a game called let-me-show-you-that-I'm-a-good-Christian, and the game is killing a lot of Christians who have left the fellowship because they simply couldn't play the game anymore.

Am I saying that Christians ought to be as bad as they can in order to be as honest as they can? Am I saying that we ought to amend the old hymn to read "I am sinking deep in sin, and isn't it fun?" Of course not. If you can't say, with John Wesley, that you are "moving toward perfection," you ought to wonder if you are the genuine article. If you don't see Christ making you more loving, kind, and compassionate than you were last year, there is something seriously wrong. Purity and holiness are important, but if you have to fake it for either pagans or Christians, that sin is greater than the lack of purity. Let God worry about what the pagans and the Christians think—you worry about what God thinks.

Believing We're Responsible for Everything

The third reason we say yes when we ought to say no is that we believe the lie found in the oft-quoted cliché, "If you aren't a part of the solution, you are a part of the problem." That, when you think about it, is a dumb statement. It presupposes that by not being a part of the solution to the problems of the world, you have somehow caused them. Such an idea is pure nonsense (and before I was a Christian I had better words to describe it).

I am not a very good house fixer. When something goes wrong at our house, my wife calls someone to fix it before I see it. After twenty-five years of marriage, she has learned that if I touch it, I'm going to make it worse. Do you know the best thing that I can do to make things run smoothly at our house? I can stay away from whatever is broken. What is often a simple and inexpensive repair can become, with a little help from me, a major "budget-busting" expense.

A lot of Christians have not learned that about life. Sometimes the best solution is to leave a problem alone. Have you ever met those Christians who feel that every time there is a broken marriage, it is their responsibility to fix it? In most of those cases, they grease the tracks to the divorce court. May God save us from "do-gooders" who have absolutely no belief that God is capable of fixing anything without their help.

I do a lot of counseling, and I am not a counselor. However, after some twenty-two years as a pastor, I have learned, slowly, some important lessons. The hardest part about counseling is learning to be quiet when God is doing something important. I am an encourager. God has given me the gift of being a cheerleader for other Christians. Because that's the way I am, I have a tendency to want to put band-aids on cancer rather than doing the hard surgery. Time after time after listening to a problem, I have wanted to say, "Don't worry. It's going to be okay." I am learning, however, that when God is doing surgery, I am not to interfere. In other words, I am learning to trust God.

You can't say no to good things unless you have learned to trust the sovereignty of God. It is only because He is God that I can sleep at night. Bill Schaffer, the director of music and the arts at the church I serve, once told me after a very pressurized time at the church, "Steve, if I didn't believe that God was in charge of all of this mess, I would jump off the nearest bridge."

There are so many people in the world who will try, sometimes without meaning to, to manipulate you. They are everywhere, and you have to be careful—the television preachers who tell you their minis-try is going to come tumbling down if you don't send money; the committee chairman who thinks that when Christ returns, He will come first to that committee meeting; the religious leader who has a tendency to get a willing horse (a Christian who says yes all the time) and ride him till he dies; the parent who tells you that you couldn't possibly be a good son or daughter unless you call eight times a day; the social activist who makes you believe you are personally respon-sible for every social ill; and even sometimes the author (like me) who makes you feel you have to say no all the time.

Learn to say no to the manipulators. If you don't, you will never learn to be obedient to the only One before whom you are always required to say yes.

Norm Evans, who heads a ministry to athletes, told about a new lineman with a professional football team who, during the first game in which he played, had a problem with the opposing lineman. He finally went to the coach and said, "Coach, he keeps pulling my helmet over my eyes. What should I do?"

The coach replied, just as our Coach replies, *"Don't let him do it."*

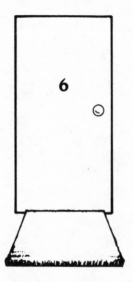

"He has delivered us from the power of darkness and translated us into the king-dom of the Son of His love, in whom we have redemption through His blood, the forgiveness of sins."

COLOSSIANS 1:13–14

The Great Manipulator, Part 1

6

I live in a rather affluent area of the country, and sometimes when I see all that I have, I feel guilty. I have noticed that the more I acquire, the more time I must expend to protect all my acquisitions. In other words, I have lots of stuff, and I am getting to the point of spending much of my time protecting my stuff. Don't be so shocked. The Father is dealing with me, and I am learning, by His grace, to work toward simplicity in my life. I know all the things Jesus said about the rich, and I know the dangers of modern-day materialism.

The point is that when you have much, you feel compassion for those who have little. And it is a very small step from compassion to guilt. One of the most interesting phenomena of our time is the "political left" bias of the wealthy. The spectrum runs from the wealthy suburbanite who has a plan to distribute everybody else's wealth, to the "radical chic" of New York and Los Angeles, to the daughter of wealthy parents who, feeling guilty for the wealth in which she has grown up, becomes an expert on making bombs to kill the bourgeoisie.

Please understand that I am not making a political statement. That isn't the issue here. Because Hitler believed the multiplication tables does not make the multiplication tables wrong. The point is that a lot of the political left, when seen among the wealthy, is the result of guilt and not the result of rational process of thought.

A number of years ago Rusty Anderson, a stockbroker friend of mine, and I decided that we needed to minister to the poor. We prayed about it and decided that when we ministered to the poor, we shouldn't be in the position of a leader. What we needed to do was to really get down and do some manual labor—to, as it were, "get our hands dirty" with and for the poor.

Rusty had a friend who was a Salvation Army officer, and he said that he would ask his friend if there were something we could do to help him out. The Salvation Army officer was surprised, but he accepted our offer to do some work around the Salvation Army. After all, it wasn't often that a stockbroker and a Presbyterian pastor made that kind of offer.

Early one Saturday morning Rusty and I, dressed in our dirty jeans and old shirts, made our way to "minister to the poor." When I picked Rusty up that morning, he told me he didn't know exactly where we were going but that he was sure it was down in the slums. So we headed for the ghetto, checked the address, and found that it was not right in the ghetto, but farther out. We got on the right street and started counting numbers. The closer we got to the right number, the better the neighborhood looked. In fact, we started going by some places that made *us* look poor.

By the time we got to the Salvation Army church, we were in the suburbs, and (I suspect that this is the exception for most Salvation Army works) it was a magnificent building with landscaped grounds more beautiful than the buildings and grounds of some of the wealthiest churches in Miami.

But we had promised, so we reported to Rusty's friend and began to work. I was given a lawn mower, and Rusty some hedge clippers. Every time I pushed my lawn mower past Rusty, who was clipping the hedge, we would break out in gales of laughter. How silly we looked! What idiots we had made of ourselves in our efforts to "help the poor."

Rusty and I have laughed about that incident a number of times over the years. We are a little bit wiser now and a lot older, and one of the things we have come to realize is that there is great motivating power in guilt. Let's talk about it.

GUILT AS A MOTIVATOR

A number of years ago, a study was done on people who had entered "full-time"Christian service. The object of the study was to determine the psychological motives for entering a religious profession. Interestingly, the study revealed that a great majority of people who serve in full-time religious jobs were there because of guilt. In other words, guilt was the motivating factor.

I suspect that if we were to do a similar study on laymen and laywomen in the church, we would find that there, too, one of the significant motivating factors in their decision to be in the church was a high degree of guilt.

Don't get me wrong. I believe we are guilty. The Bible says, "For when we were still without strength, in due time Christ died for the ungodly. For scarcely for a righteous man will one die; yet perhaps for a good man someone would even dare to die. But God demonstrates His own love toward us, in that while we were still sinners, Christ died for us" (Rom. 5:6–8). Jeremiah 17:9 says, "The heart is deceitful above all things, and desperately wicked; Who can know it?"

I used to believe that there were two kinds of people in the world:

the good and the bad. The bad people drank too much, cursed too much, smoked too much, and mowed their lawns on Sunday. The good people didn't drink too much, curse too much, or smoke too much, and they went to church on Sunday. I was not a pastor for very long before I found out that there are indeed two kinds of people in the world. The types are different, however, from what I had supposed. I found that there are bad people who know it and bad people who don't know it. The bad people who know it and want to do something about it are in the church, and the bad people who think they are good have no use for Christ or the church.

Jesus said, "Those who are well have no need of a physician, but those who are sick. . . . For I did not come to call the righteous, but sinners, to repentance" (Matt. 9:12–13). In other words, if you are following Christ, you do so because you are a sinner, not because you aren't. The church is a fellowship of people who have been forgiven and are in the process of change.

Thus it is only natural that one would find Christians who are aware of their sin in the church and in positions of leadership of the church. Guilt is certainly a proper factor in people's coming to Christ—maybe the only legitimate one. The essence of the Christian faith is a paradox which says that in order to qualify for it you have to admit you're unqualified for it.

But in this chapter I'm not talking about forgiven sinners; I'm talking about forgiven sinners who either don't "feel" forgiven or who act as if they aren't forgiven. If you fall into that category, you are vulnerable to every religious huckster and con man who comes down the pike. It is open season on guilt-ridden Christians, and that makes me angry. It makes me angry at the religious hucksters and con men who use guilt to motivate, and it also makes me angry when I or other people in my family allow ourselves to be manipulated by guilt. I want to cry out with Paul:

> O foolish Galatians! Who has bewitched you that you should not obey the truth, before whose eyes Jesus Christ was clearly portrayed among you as

crucified? This only I want to learn from you: Did you receive the Spirit by the works of the law, or by the hearing of faith? Are you so foolish? Having begun in the Spirit, are you now being made perfect by the flesh? (Gal. 3:1–3).

HOW GUILT WORKS

If we are going to talk about guilt, it would be good to find out what it is. The *Psychiatric Dictionary* (4th edition) gives the following definition:

> Realization that one has done wrong by violating some ethical, moral or religious principle. Associated with such realization typically are lowered self-esteem and a feeling that one should expiate or make retribution for the wrong that has been done.
>
> As used in psychoanalytic writings, the term usually refers to neurotic, unreasonable, or pathologic guilt feelings that do not appear to be justified by the reasons adduced for the guilt.[1]

Now, in order to understand how guilt works, let me give you a highly simplified four-step description of the *healthy* way to deal with guilt. First, there is the violation of a standard. That standard can be a biblical standard, a personal moral code, or a code one has accepted from one's peers. Whatever the standard, there is a real violation that begins the movement toward guilt. For instance, a little girl gets dressed in a new dress. Her mother says to her, "Now honey, you be careful and keep the dress clean." Then suppose the little girl promptly goes out and gets mud on the new dress. She knows that she has violated her mother's standard.

Second, there is the legitimate feeling of guilt. That feeling is the unease we feel when we know something is wrong, that we have fallen short, that we have missed the mark. One of the most dangerous practices in which some people engage is the practice of denying the legitimate feeling of guilt. When I have violated God's standards (or, for that matter, my own best standards), I ought to feel guilty. Unless I accurately identify what the feeling of unease is, I will not be able to do anything about alleviating the unease. A sense of guilt in the face of the violation of legitimate standards is legitimate guilt. To continue the illustration, the little girl says, "I should not have been playing in the mud, but I did and now my dress is dirty. I feel bad about my dress getting dirty."

Third, there is the need for punishment, forgiveness, or retribution. One of the great mistakes we have made in our penal system is the one-sided emphasis on rehabilitation. It would be far healthier psychologically if we balanced punishment with rehabilitation. Prison ought to be seen as paying the price or balancing the books. The little girl shows her dress to her mother, and her mother either spanks her or forgives her.

Finally, there is the freedom from guilt. After one has done something wrong, felt guilty about it, and received punishment, forgiveness, or retribution, one is then free of the guilt. Our little girl, after her spanking, is a very happy little girl because she doesn't feel bad about herself. She has paid the price, and now she can go on about her business until the next time (and there *will* be a next time), when she gets her dress dirty.

What I've described above is a perfectly healthy way to deal with guilt. We have all used that system, even without knowing it, to deal with our own guilt. For Christians, the third step was the action of Christ. He died for our sins, and as a result we have forgiveness and can be free.

ILLEGITIMATE GUILT

The problem comes when the first step is not an actual violation of a definable standard. In other words, if we feel guilty when we are not objectively guilty, the system doesn't work. What one does when there has been no legitimate violation and there are still feelings of guilt is to go back and forth between steps two and three without ever feeling free.

Let me illustrate what I mean. A number of years ago I spent considerable time counseling Sally, a young woman who had become a prostitute. She didn't like herself and she didn't like her profession, but after repeated attempts to change, she told me that it was no use, and she gave up.

Let me tell you Sally's story. When Sally was a year old, her mother had a lobotomy (i.e., a psychosurgical procedure). The surgery left her mother without the ability to function, so she was placed in an institution for custodial care for the rest of her life. Sally's father, knowing there was no way he could work and take care of his daughter, placed Sally with two maiden aunts.

A one-year-old child doesn't have the ability to reason. But my friend could feel, and her feelings were, "I used to have a mother who loved me. She left me. My father loved me too, and he got rid of me. There must be something very wrong with me." In other words, Sally had significant feelings of guilt, yet she had not violated any standard.

I talked to another young girl whose mother was raped. The girl I counseled had absolutely nothing to do with the situation. She was asleep in her room when the incident happened. When I first talked to her, however, she was quick to assert that she had opened the door to the rapist. Somehow, because the incident was understandably traumatic to the mother and caused the mother to turn in on herself, my friend began to think, I *must have had something to do with the rape*. It was a short step from that feeling to the belief that she had actually opened the door to the rapist when she had not.

There was also the teenager whose father was killed in an automobile accident. The father and son relationship was rather strained, as is often the case during a son's adolescence. When I talked to the young man, he told me he was responsible for his father's accident. He wasn't, but he had feelings of guilt.

There was the father who told me, after his wife died, that he had trouble dealing with the guilt he felt. I asked him why he felt guilty, and he told me he didn't know, but he did.

When my own parents would have an argument during my childhood, I used to wonder what was wrong with me. Of course, nothing was wrong with me. I wasn't the one doing the arguing, but I still felt guilty. People are my business, and over and over again I have encountered Christians who feel guilty without having violated any standard.

When the feelings of guilt are not related to the reality of violation, one still tries to resolve the guilt in a healthy way (i.e., punishment, forgiveness, or retribution). Because there is no legitimate violation, there is never freedom. One simply feels more and more guilty and tries to resolve the greater guilt with the same method. In other words, we set up situations in which we are punished; we are constantly seeking forgiveness and forever trying to "balance the books."

Are you constantly "putting yourself down?" Do you sometimes say to yourself, "I'm just a klutz. I never do anything right"? Do you spend much of your time apologizing to other people? Have you confessed a particular sin to God a thousand times wondering when He is going to forgive you? Do you constantly find yourself in the predicament where you get hurt? Are you always afraid to confront other people with a difficult truth? When you are accused of something, do you always assume you are at fault? Do you always dread disagreements? Are you always defending yourself against some real or imagined wrong? When a clerk in a department store is rude to you, do you wonder what you did wrong? Whenever your pastor preaches on almost any sin, do you find yourself blushing? When you read the Bible, do you find yourself always underlining the passages that deal with sin and failure? Do you sometimes get to the edge of success and then do something stupid to ruin it? Do you find yourself embarrassed by compliments and ill at ease when others praise you?

If you have answered any of the above questions in the affirmative, you likely have a problem with illegitimate guilt. (If you answered none of the above questions in the affirmative, then you will probably lie about other things too.) As a matter of fact, we all carry some emotional baggage around. Because that is true, we are vulnerable to the manipulation of guilt to the degree that we are suffering from illegitimate guilt.

HOW TO HANDLE ILLEGITIMATE GUILT

The question that immediately comes to mind is this: What do I do about it? Unfortunately, there is no system in which you can just go through the right steps and are thereby freed from illegitimate guilt. It is a lifelong struggle for many of us. However, there are some guidelines that can help.

Understand the Standard

First, you can make sure you understand the standard. In other words, you can be aware of the standard by which you measure yourself and understand the specifics of that standard. Because I am a Christian, the Bible is my standard. It is my responsibility to *know* what the Bible says in regard to how I act, think, work, and believe. I know that the Bible tells me I ought to be truthful. When I am not truthful, because I know what the standard is, I feel guilty. At that point I ought to be guilty because I have violated my standard.

A man who has a reputation for being a Christian once called me and asked if he could have a few minutes of my time. He said he was dealing with a difficult problem and needed some help. When he came into my study, he wasted no time in getting down to the problem. He said, "Pastor, I don't want to waste your time or mine. I am trying to determine what God would have me do about my mistress."

I asked him, "You mean that you are trying to find enough emotional power to say no to that particular sin?"

"No," he said, "I am trying to act in a loving way. I love my wife and I love my mistress, and I want to do the Christian thing."

I asked him if he believed the Bible and wanted to govern his life accordingly. He replied that of course he believed the Bible because he was a Christian.

107

Yet, his standard was not the Bible. When I took him to a number of biblical texts that dealt with his specific actions, he rejected what the Bible had to say. He said that his standard was the Bible, but his real standard was either self-gratification or some kind of nebulous definition of love. He had not clearly decided on his standard.

We often say that we accept the Bible as our standard when in reality our standard is the approval of our peers, the pleasure of our mother, or the accumulation of wealth. It is important that, as Christians, we understand that our only legitimate standard is the Bible, and then when we violate it, we can deal with the violation in a healthy way.

Face the Reality of the Fall

Second, in order to deal with illegitimate guilt, one needs to face the reality of the Fall. In other words, one needs to recognize that perfection is impossible in government, in education, in the church, and in one's heart. Political statism (i.e., the view that advocates heavy involvement of the state in the control, especially economic, of the country) is a fallacy because it is based on the untruth that government is perfectable. Perfectionism in the church creates more guilt than sin and can destroy Christians. I have a Catholic priest friend who has a card he sometimes gives people. On one side is written, "Bless those who curse you . . ." On the other side: ". . . because they may be right."

I have written in the back of my Bible, "You wouldn't be so shocked at your own sin if you didn't have such a high opinion of yourself." I sometimes flip to the back of my Bible and read that just before I preach. It helps me deal with my real sins and also the vague feeling of guilt that I can't attach to any biblical standard I have violated.

An old, wise statement makes the point well: "There is so much bad in the best of us and so much good in the worst of us that it ill behooves any of us to judge the rest of us." That philosophy ought to be applied to oneself as well.

Understand please, that I'm not excusing sin. I am, rather, defining reality. When one experiences feelings of illegitimate guilt, one ought to be able to say to oneself, "Of course I feel guilty. Some of it is deserved, and I have been forgiven and am getting better. Other times I feel guilty when I ought not to feel guilty. I'm also forgiven for feeling guilty when I ought not to feel guilty. Therefore, I don't have to feel guilty."

Discover the Sources

Third, one ought to try to discover the sources of illegitimate guilt. Ask the Father why you feel so inferior to other people, why you always assume you are wrong, why you are afraid to confront, and why you care so much what people think about you. Then be silent before the Father and allow Him to draw up the memories that He can heal. Perhaps you need, if it is a major problem, to talk to your pastor or a wise friend. An alcoholic parent, a traumatic sexual experience, a cruel comment made to you when you were a child, an overemphasis on perfection, or a recurring physical sickness are just a few of the areas where we can begin to develop feelings of guilt that are not related to reality. Allow the Father to bring them to memory, and then begin to deal with them by asking Him to take the memories He shows you. One of the interesting aspects about debilitating memories is that they die (or almost die) in the light.

Appreciate God's Grace

Fourth, in dealing with illegitimate guilt, one must have a high (i.e., biblical) view of God's grace. Too many Christians speak biblical doctrine with their mouths and live the American folk religion with their lives. The Bible says, "For by grace you have been saved through faith, and that not of yourselves; it is the gift of God" (Eph. 2:8). In Romans 5:20b Paul wrote, "But where sin abounded, grace abounded much more."

Someone tells the story about the man who went to heaven and

NO MORE MR. NICE GUY!

was thereupon confronted by Peter, who said to the man, "In order to get into heaven you must have one thousand points. What have you done to earn your one thousand points?"

The man said, "I never heard that before, but I'm sure I have earned at least that many. I am the father of three children, and I have been a good father and husband. I have never cheated on my wife or mistreated my children. One of my boys is a pastor, another a missionary, and my daughter is a nurse working in the slums of our city. I am a banker, and I give over 20 percent of my income to the Lord's work. But I don't just give money, I put my life and my words where my money is. In my bank I have worked to bring low income housing to the poor in my city. I spend one night a week working in a clinic in the slums. I have put a number of poor kids through college, and I support a number of missionaries on the field. Every Christmas I go with the Salvation Army in our city to help them raise money. I always support my pastor and his work for the Lord, and I have been an elder in our church almost all of my adult life. Most of my deeds are done in secret, and I have built, anonymously, an educational wing of our church and a hospital in Haiti."

The man looked over to Peter and said, "How am I doing?"

Peter replied, "Well, that's one point. Have you done anything else?"

"Good night!" the man exclaimed. "God have mercy!"

Peter laughed and said, "You've got it! That's a thousand points. Come on in."

It is good sometimes to reflect deeply on the grace of God. His grace is absolutely sufficient. He has done everything necessary to make us acceptable, and we *are* therefore acceptable. Paul Tournier, in his old but good book *Guilt and Grace*, has made the point that true guilt and false (i.e., illegitimate) guilt can be separated by knowing that true guilt is a violation of God's standards and false guilt violates man's standards. He then goes on to make a very profound statement:

"Therefore, real guilt is often something quite different from that which constantly weighs us down, because of our fear of social judgment and the disapproval of men. *We become independent of them in proportion as we depend on God*"[2] (italics mine). The more we concentrate on the grace of God, and the less we concentrate on ourselves, the freer we become.

Act Forgiven

Finally, in dealing with illegitimate guilt one needs to learn to follow the advice given to John Wesley, "Fake it till you make it." (Well, that isn't exactly the advice he was given, but it's close.) Wesley was once in great difficulty because he didn't believe in the concept of faith. He went to his spiritual advisor, who said, "Wesley, preach faith until you have faith, and then because you have faith you will preach faith." That means that Wesley was asked to fake it until he made it.

Now lest you accuse me of advocating hypocrisy, let me suggest that I am not advocating hypocrisy but obedience. If you were free from debilitating guilt, if you thought you had been made worthy by the blood of Christ, if you knew you were free of feelings of unworthiness, what would you do? Do it. Why? Because, if you are a Christian, you are, in fact, free from guilt and worthy. By conforming to a reality instead of a lie, you will come to reflect in your feelings, as well as your life, the reality of a forgiven sinner who is clean.

In the next chapter we are going to deal with the manipulation that is possible because of guilt. For now let me say that the Christian who is manipulated by guilt (either legitimate or illegitimate) is denying the very reality of his or her life. Please don't allow the death of Christ to be wasted.

Evangelist Leighton Ford told about a man who owned a Rolls Royce. While traveling on vacation, there was a mechanical failure. The man called the company from which he had bought the car, and they flew in a mechanic from England to repair it. After waiting a number of weeks for a bill for the repair job, the man wrote to the company in England and asked for a bill. He received a telex. It read: "We have no record of a Rolls Royce with a mechanical failure."

Because of the death of Christ, the Christian stands clean before the God of the universe. An understanding of that fact is absolutely necessary if any Christian is going to stand against the pagan and religious manipulation of our time. When we who trust in the atoning work of Christ go before the judgment seat of God, He will say, "I have no record of the failure."

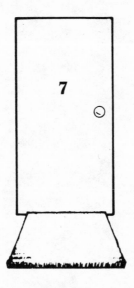

"And do not be conformed to this world, but be transformed by the renewing of your mind, that you may prove what is that good and acceptable and perfect will of God."

ROMANS 12:2

The Great Manipulator, Part 2

7

In the last chapter, we talked about guilt and what it is. Now let's talk about what it does in terms of the general subject of Christian boldness. It would be wonderful if we could say, "Okay, I suffer from guilt. Big deal! Some of it is real guilt because I have done some bad things, some of it is false guilt. So, what else is new? I'm only human. I will ask God to forgive me and I will be free. Then I will, by His grace, get better and better every day in every way."

As a matter of fact, that would be one healthy way of dealing with the problem. However, it isn't that simple. Guilt isn't like the measles. You don't deal with it once and then it's over. All of us all our lives deal with real and false guilt, and there is no magic formula we can use that will eliminate our participation in this human dilemma.

In this chapter I want to say a word about sin and guilt, and then I want to give a list of biblical okays for the Christian who is not manipulated by guilt.

THE IMPORTANCE OF BALANCE

First, let me say something about sin. No Christian has a right to be flippant about sin. I'm a Bible teacher, and one of the difficulties of teaching is maintaining balance. Human beings have an amazing proclivity toward imbalance. A cult is not usually a group of people who have it all wrong. Rather, they are often people who have taken one truth to the exclusion of all other truths, or who have taken one truth so far down the road that it has gone beyond its destination.

Another illustration of this point may be seen in the Science of the Mind groups who have said some positive things. For instance, Christian Science teaches that God is sovereign. Its adherents are quick to point out that the Christian faith is not dualistic (i.e., there are not two equal and opposing forces of good and evil). That is biblically true. Throughout Scripture, God makes quite clear that Satan is a created being and that he is only, in the ultimate sense, a lackey of God. In the first chapter of Job, you will remember, before Satan could touch Job he had to ask God's permission. First John 4:4 says, "He who is in you [God's Spirit] is greater than he [Satan] who is in the world."

It is one thing, however, to say that Christianity is not dualistic, and it is quite another to say that Satan, evil, sin, and sickness are not "real," as the Christian Scientists do. The cultic nature of Christian Science is not in the basic truth but in the taking of that truth to the exclusion of all other truth. Balance is terribly important.

I was speaking to the singles group in the church I serve about the subject of this book. I asked for comments on some of the topics I would be covering here. I heard over and over again from those folks that it was important that I maintain balance. To call Christians to be bold, they said, is quite another matter than to call Christians to become a "pain in the neck." Gentleness is a gift of the Spirit, and it is important that gentleness not be defined away in my definition of boldness. Just as they pointed out that gentleness must be in the "mix" of boldness, they also pointed out that it would be dangerous,

116

in my effort to keep Christians from acting out of guilt, to ignore what the Bible says about sin. It is one thing to say that a Christian is forgiven, and it is quite another to say that sin is unimportant.

So, in an effort to keep the balance, I want to write a word of caution about sin. I believe that the problem with most Christians is not the problem of sin but the problem of forgiveness. Psychologically, one would sin less if one understood forgiveness. The whole thrust of Romans is that everybody has an "authority" problem. When the law says that we must do something or that we must not do something, there is something inside us that responds, "Oh yeah, just watch me." We are constantly, as it were, "banging" up against the wall of the law. Paul said in Romans that the wall has been removed. There is nothing to "bang" against! He stated, "For when we were in the flesh, the passions of sins which were aroused by the law were at work in our members to bear fruit to death. But now we have been delivered from the law, having died to what we were held by, so that we should serve in the newness of the Spirit and not in the oldness of the letter" (Rom. 7:5–6).

THE FUTILITY OF WILL POWER

Most Christians are trying to be good by their own efforts because a Christian is supposed to be good. A Christian *is* supposed to be righteous. The problem comes when the goodness is a result of nothing but will power. We never have enough will power. Paul said, "For I know that in me (that is, in my flesh) nothing good dwells; for to will is present with me, but how to perform what is good I do not find. For the good that I will to do, I do not do; but the evil I will not to do, that I practice" (Rom. 7:18–19). And then Paul cried out (just as every Christian cries out when he or she has only willed to be good), "O wretched man that I am! Who will deliver me from this body of death?" (Rom. 7:24).

If some of what I am going to say in this chapter seems to be minimizing sin, you simply have not understood. Sin cost Christ the cross, and it would be nothing but blasphemy for me to make light of something that cost that much. Goodness is not only achieved by giving up something; it is also achieved by getting hold of something. We have come to focus too much on the sin and not enough on the Savior.

There is a young man in our church who became a Christian when he was only six. During his teen years he rebelled against his Christian faith. One time he told me that it was easy to be a Christian when he was six "because you don't have that much to give up when you are six." Listen! We have put too much emphasis on "giving up." I'm not advocating a passive acceptance of sin; however, I am advocating an active dependence on Christ.

So, some of the things I am going to be saying here may make me seem a libertine. I'm not. I simply believe that the way of righteousness comes by faith and not by hustle. Christians who work too hard at goodness often end up with the opposite result. Almost everything of any worth is a side-benefit of something else. Happiness can't be chased down, for instance, and made your own. Happiness is a side-benefit of obedience. Just so, righteousness can't be chased down either; it is a side-benefit of falling in love with Christ.

HOW GUILT IS USED TO MANIPULATE

Let's now turn to the subject of how the hucksters and the con men manipulate us with guilt. P. T. Bauer, one of the world's leading economists, professor of Economics at the London School of Economics, and fellow at Cambridge University, has written:

> Acceptance of emphatic routine allegations that the West is responsible for Third World poverty reflects and reinforces Western feelings of guilt. It has enfeebled Western diplomacy, both towards the ideologically much more aggressive Soviet bloc and also towards the Third World. And the West has come to abase itself before countries with negligible resources and no real power. Yet the allegations can be shown to be without foundation. They are readily accepted because the Western public has little firsthand knowledge of

the Third World, and because of wide-spread feelings of guilt. The West has never had it so good, and has never felt so bad about it.[1]

That is a great comment about what guilt can do to a nation, and it can affect individual Christians in just the same way. One could say about most Christians what Bauer said about the United States. We have never had it so good, and we have probably never felt so bad about it. Because there are so many people who know how bad we feel about it, it has become open season on Christians who haven't dealt with their guilt.

For the remainder of this chapter, I want to give you a list (and I'm sure that you can add to it) of those areas where you are now free to be free because you are no longer open to the manipulation of guilt. I believe that Christians should act on the known facts, and the known fact in this case is that you don't have to be guilty about certain areas of your life. What you feel is irrelevant when what you feel is not correlated by the facts you know.

A couple of years ago I went through a horrible guilt trip. A part of my ministry entails considerable travel. When you are the pastor of a local church and you are away a lot, you begin to feel guilty because you can't always do what most people expect a pastor to do. It got so bad that I went to the elders of the church and said to them, "Guys, I'm afraid that you aren't getting what you have every right to expect from a pastor. Let me suggest that we set a date for my resignation and make a smooth transition to another man who will be able to be here full-time."

Those men mean more to me than I can ever tell you. Their love and support are great gifts the Father has given me. That night, after a long discussion and a lot of prayer, those men said to me, "Pastor, we believe that God called you to be our pastor. Further, we believe that God called you to serve Him in the places around the country where you speak. We are only being obedient to God in affirming both of those ministries and in supporting you in every way we can." Because of that meeting, the structure of the Key Biscayne Presbyterian Church became somewhat different from that of most churches. It is a structure designed to give their pastor the freedom to be what God called him to be. I left that meeting feeling like a new man. The unanimous vote of confidence from the elders was a wonderful gift.

The problem was, I still felt guilty.

So, I called Stuart Briscoe, who has dealt with this same problem most of his ministry, and asked for his help. He said, "Steve, have you cleared this dual ministry with the elders of the church?" I told him about the meeting, and he said, "Then the guilt you are feeling doesn't come from God. You are creating it for yourself. Act in a manner consistent with what you know to be true."

That was good advice, and it is the same advice I want to give you in some particular areas. The primary fact I want you to remember is that you are not guilty, or at least you don't *have* to be guilty. If that is true, certain premises follow. Let's check them out.

WHAT IT'S OKAY TO BE

It's Okay to Be Human

First, it's okay to be human. Most Christians don't believe that being human ought to be on their agenda. In some circles it almost goes without saying that "real men don't eat quiche," and real Christians don't sin (or, if they do, they can't let anyone know). Nonsense! High, unrealistic expectations can kill you. They are far more dangerous to your health than cigarettes. God works in a process, and if you have the expectation of being at the end of the process before you have gone through the process, you are going to suffer great disappointment. The slogan "Be patient, God isn't through with me yet" is not only a slogan; it is a truth that every healthy Christian must understand with his or her mind, heart, and soul.

120

Perfection is not attainable in this world. If you think it is, you are going to end up a neurotic Christian. The cartoonist who showed a cannibal pouring the contents of a small box labeled "Instant Missionary" into a big pot is not the only one dreaming. We all dream about instant goodness, instant power, and instant perfection. It simply doesn't work that way. While you ought to feel properly guilty when you don't measure up to God's standard, you ought to be properly relieved to know that you didn't surprise God when you didn't measure up to His standard, and that He has made provision for you at the foot of the cross.

When I was growing up, the sentence I heard probably more than any other was this: "Stephen is not living up to his potential." That was true, of course. It always was true; it is still true; it always will be true (until I become like Him in heaven). There is always more that I could do. I could always be better than I am. I could always love Him more and serve Him better.

Now, when my brothers and sisters in Christ motivate me to a better walk with Christ by reminding me that I'm really not trying very hard, they have done me a service. However, when they have selfish, vested interest in their motivation of me, it ceases to be motivation and becomes manipulation. "The search for excellence" can be a joyous experience of growing. That is the way it ought to be with people who follow Christ. However, that same search can become a constant reminder of my lack of excellence, and when that happens I become quite vulnerable to manipulation.

The writer of Hebrews, who spoke about the sacrificial system in the old covenant, points to the difference between the sacrifice of Christ, once and for all, and the sacrifices that had to be made in the temple. Then he says, "*But in those sacrifices there is a reminder of sins every year*" (Heb. 10:3, italics mine). In other words, we don't need to be reminded over and over that we are sinners who fall short. The death of Christ removed the need to be constantly reminded.

> Therefore, brethren, having boldness to enter the Holiest by the blood of Jesus, by a new and living way which He consecrated for us, through the veil, that is, His flesh, and having a High Priest over the house of God, let us draw near with a true heart in full assurance of faith, having our hearts sprinkled from an evil conscience and our bodies washed with pure water. Let us hold fast the confession of our hope without wavering, for He who promised is faithful (Heb. 10:19–23).

Let me give you a literal translation from the original Greek of the above. "Don't bug me. I have been forgiven!"

The next time someone tells you that you aren't living up to your potential, and you perceive that he or she is trying to get you to do something, reply, "Of course I'm not living up to my potential. If it's okay with you, I think I won't live up to it for a while longer."

It's Okay to Be Right

Second, if you're not guilty, it is okay to be right. One of the great weapons used by manipulators is the knowledge that if they sound right, those who are suffering from guilt will assume they *are* right. Recently I was speaking in one of our Christian colleges, and a student who appeared to be very upset asked if he could speak to me. We made an appointment, and as soon as we sat down in the coffee shop he said to me, "Mr. Brown, I need some help in getting my life straightened out." I braced myself for a confession about drugs, homosexuality, or cheating on exams. What this young man said surprised me: "Mr. Brown, I have to deal with my arrogance and pride."

As I looked at this young man across the table from me, his head bowed, his spirit broken, and his eyes welling up with tears, I thought to myself, *He may have a lot of things wrong with him, but arrogance and pride aren't on the list*. So I asked him how he knew that he was arrogant and prideful. He told me about a small group of Christians with whom he met regularly. One of the tenets of the small group was total honesty, and the week before, the group had decided to be totally honest with him. The whole meeting had been devoted to a discussion of what was wrong with him. It all boiled down to his arrogant and prideful attitude.

I said, "Have you ever considered that they were wrong about you?" From the look on his face, it was clear that he hadn't. I continued, "I suspect that, given the fact that you are human, there must be some elements of pride in your life, but from this short time of knowing you, I don't see that as your glaring sin."

We talked for almost two hours. At the end of the time, he decided that maybe the group was wrong. But the fact is he had a horrible struggle because of his guilt. He had assumed that if someone said something untrue about him, he had to change. W. B. Yeats understood:

> Come, fix upon me that accusing eye.
> I thirst for accusation.[2]

R. C. Sproul, one of the finest Christian writers of our time, was told by a teacher that he couldn't write. That teacher almost robbed us of some great books because, for a long time, R. C. believed her. It is the same with many of us. Time after time I have seen Christians failing because they believed the turkeys who told them they were dumb.

Maybe you have been told you're dumb. Did you ever think that the people who told you that could be wrong? Perhaps you are afraid to articulate your ideas because you have been told that your ideas aren't worth much. Did you ever think that the idea that your ideas aren't worth much isn't worth much? Perhaps you don't need to apologize all the time. Have you ever considered that one doesn't need to apologize when one is right? Have you ever entertained the idea that you were right?

Tolerance is a good word, but if we aren't very careful we can allow tolerance to become a lack of conviction. Early in the ecumenical movement, it was "in" to have ecumenical dialogues. I wanted to be "in," so I arranged an ecumenical dialogue at the little church on Cape

Cod I was then serving. I had a panel of Catholic priests and Protestant ministers. About halfway through the meeting, I had decided that there weren't really many differences between Catholics and Protestants.

Dr. John Stanton, my beloved mentor and a participant on the panel, listened to all the dialogue and finally decided there were some things that needed to be said. "I'm glad we are here," he said, "and it gives me an opportunity to get some answers to some questions I have been asking a long time." He then proceeded, amid the shock of the assembled brethren, to list the Roman Catholic doctrines that he thought were unsound and unbiblical. In effect he said, "I think you are wrong and I am right about these things." For the first time that evening, we had real dialogue.

Christians ought to do that more often. I believe if I hear one more time, "I'm not a Baptist . . ." (or a Presbyterian or a Methodist), "I'm a Christian," I will scream. Our forefathers called that kind of statement a lack of conviction. Of course it is more important to be a Christian rather than a member of a denomination and to hold to a certain set of sectarian beliefs. But to suggest that beliefs are not important is just another way of saying, "It doesn't matter what you believe, or what your convictions are. Let's just join hands with Jesus and walk off into the sunset together."

The law of averages says that unless you are unusually dumb, you will be right 50 percent of the time when you disagree with others, even if you only guess at the answer. That means that if you are counting yourself wrong more than 50 percent of the time, it may be that you have allowed your guilt to "muddle" your brains.

It's Okay to Be Offensive (Sometimes)

Third, it is okay to be offensive (sometimes). One of the interesting phenomena of our time is the emergence of the "religious right." The criticisms directed at conservative Christians have been nothing less than hysterical. "Dangerous," "simplistic," "narrow," "divisive," "malevolent," "threatening," and "frightening" are just a few of the terms we hear applied often to those Christians who have chosen to be outspoken in their conservative political views. After reading some of the silly editorials directed at the religious right, one gets the feeling that if Christians would just stay "in their place" (i.e., say prayers and sing hymns), they wouldn't be bothered. For some reason, everybody has the right to proclaim views no matter how banal and silly, except Christians. Christians are supposed to smile, love everybody, and be nice.

I love Tony Campolo and love to be around him, but I hardly agree with any of his political or sociological views. He often offends people by what he says, and I like that even if I think he is wrong. We are brothers, and sometimes when I hear Tony speak I find myself thinking, I *don't believe he said that!* And then I look around at the way he was willing to put his views (often offensive to his audience) on the line, and I'm proud to be his friend.

Vernon Grounds once said that the trouble with some Christians is they almost say something. I don't know about you, but I'm tired of Christians who almost say something. I like Tony Campolo and Jerry Falwell because they don't "almost" say something. You know what they believe and think because they are not afraid of being offensive. They remind me of most of the good guys in the Bible.

Guilt causes many Christians to feel that because they are bad, they have to work hard at being liked. I believe that most Christians ought to try to offend someone at least once a day just to make sure they haven't sold their soul. Truth almost always offends. Jesus said, "Woe to you when all men speak well of you, for so did their fathers to the false prophets" (Luke 6:26).

It's Okay to Be Wrong

Finally, it is okay to be wrong. In fact, everything I have said above may be wrong. I am glad, however, that I said it. And, best of all, I don't feel guilty about it.

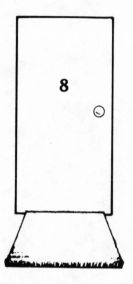

"Therefore do not worry, saying, 'What shall we eat?' or 'What shall we drink?' or 'What shall we wear?' For after all these things the Gentiles seek. For your heavenly Father knows that you need all these things. But seek first the kingdom of God and His righteousness, and all these things shall be added to you."

MATTHEW 6:31–33

The Bane
of
Boldness

8

Jean Shepherd, in a humorous and insightful article titled "The Decline and Fall of the Wimp," wrote:

> Scholars studying the field (*Wimpus apologeticus americanus*) believe the high point of wimpishness was captured by a photographer showing President Jimmy Carter seated in a rowboat fighting off an attacking killer rabbit with an oar. From that moment on, wimps were in retreat, casting nervous glances behind them in fear of pursuing rabbits, while the rest of us instinctively sighed in relief, hoping that the whole madness was now exposed and would die of its own nervousness. As my Aunt Clara used to say: "My best friend, Mabel, died of nerves." I never knew what she meant, but I do now.[1]

While guilt may be the greatest motivating factor in the creation of the wimp (Shepherd says that if a plague of locusts descends on an obscure country 12,000 miles away, a wimp will ask, "How have I failed them? Where did I go wrong?"), fear and worry run a very close second.

In the parable of the talents, Jesus told us about three different reactions to the master who gave different talents to his servants while he, the master, went away. The first and the second servants went out and increased the master's money, but the third hid what the master had given him in the ground. When asked why he didn't at least invest the money and get the interest for the master, the servant replied, "I knew you to be a hard man, reaping where you have not sown, and gathering where you have not scattered seed. And I *was afraid*" (Matt. 25:24–25a, italics mine).

Fear is the bane of boldness. "I was afraid." Those words have accounted for more failure to stand where God would have the Christian stand than almost anything else. It isn't that we don't know where to stand, and it isn't that we don't want to stand. The problem is—we're afraid. We're afraid we might fail; we're afraid people may not like us; we're afraid that we might get out of the will of God; we're afraid of the wrath of God; we're afraid of what people will do to us if they get angry; we're afraid of cancer, pollution, war, and AIDS. We're afraid not to be afraid, lest in our moment of weakness we get destroyed. We're afraid of losing our material goods and our spiritual superiority. We're afraid, with Satchel Paige, to look back lest something should be gaining on us. And, most of all, we're afraid of death.

Jake Fen, a Hungarian, had a funny sense of humor. One time he came on the novel idea that he could end his wife's incessant nagging by letting her know how she would feel if he committed suicide. So Mr. Fen built an elaborate harness to make it appear as though he had hanged himself. His unsuspecting wife came in from shopping, saw her husband hanging from the rafter, let out a scream, and promptly fainted.

A neighbor, hearing the scream, came over. Finding what she logically assumed were two corpses, she took the opportunity to loot the apartment. As the neighbor was leaving, her arms laden with loot, the outraged, very alive and hanging Mr. Fen kicked her stoutly in the backside. The neighbor, knowing that dead folks don't kick that hard, promptly died of a heart attack. Mr. Fen was acquitted of manslaughter, and, at last report, Mrs. Fen was trying to forgive him.[2]

Fear can kill you. But even more important than that, fear can kill your boldness. Unless the believer can find a healthy way to deal with fear, boldness is not an option. Let's talk about it.

First, I want you to remember that fear is not, in itself, a bad thing. In fact, fear, like pain, can be God's way of turning on the warning system. Paul Brand and Philip Yancey, in their fine book *In His Image*, pointed out that leprosy is not a disease that simply causes deterioration. It also causes the loss of feeling. Often the deterioration is not because of the disease itself but because, without pain, people do things they wouldn't ordinarily do, such as placing a hand on a hot stove, gripping a saw in the wrong place, or holding a door knob too tightly. They commented, "Leprosy patients suffer because they feel no pain; they yearn for the demons who would alert them to impending danger."[3]

Just as pain is a gift of God to warn us of a problem, so fear can be a gift of God that enables us to stay out of trouble or, when we are in trouble, "stirs up the juices" in our bodies so we can act appropriately. That great "theologian" Fran Tarkenton once said, "Fear causes people to draw back from situations; it brings on mediocrity; it dulls creativity; it sets one up to be a loser in life." That, of course, is true, but it is important to see the other side of the picture. Fear causes people to draw back from dangerous situations; it brings on mediocrity, but it also challenges us to greatness; it dulls creativity, but it also produces it; it sets one up to be a loser in life, but it also makes for winners. Fran Tarkenton would be the first to admit that without fear his record-setting football career would have been something less than it was.

Someone tells the story about the two men who were out walking in the woods when they heard the roar of a grizzly bear. Both men were frightened, and with reason. One man promptly sat down and started putting on his running shoes. The other said to him, "Jim, you don't think you're going to outrun that bear, do you?"

Jim replied, "Of course I'm not going to outrun that bear. I don't have to. I just have to outrun you."

USING FEAR TO YOUR ADVANTAGE

Fear is sometimes a great and good motivator. The question then is not how does one get rid of fear, but how does one use fear to one's advantage?

Let's turn to an incident in the incarnational life of Jesus for some answers. In the fourth chapter of Mark, Jesus was tired and was trying to get a little rest by moving away from the multitude. Mark wrote:

> On the same day, when evening had come, He said to them, "Let us cross over to the other side." Now when they had left the multitude, they took Him along in the boat as He was. And other little boats were also with Him. And a great windstorm arose, and the waves beat into the boat, so that it was already filling. But He was in the stern, asleep on a pillow. And they awoke Him and said to Him, "Teacher, do You not care that we are perishing?" Then He arose and rebuked the wind, and said to the sea, "Peace, be still!" And the wind ceased and there was a great calm. But He said to them, "Why are you so fearful? How is it that you have no faith?" And they feared exceedingly, and said to one another, "Who can this be, that even the wind and the sea obey Him!" (Mark 4:35–41).

There are a number of items in that text that are relevant to our discussion. First, you need to note that the disciples were afraid, and with good reason. At the Sea of Galilee, there are air currents that cause the wind to sweep down the narrow ravines descending to the shore from the surrounding hills. Those wind storms come with tremendous force and violence. The storms come up literally "out of the blue," and many sailors have died in them.

George Bowman told about a group of university students from Toronto who went up to Georgian Bay for a fishing trip. They hired a boat and a captain to take them out. When they were out on the water a tremendous storm arose, and the captain sat at the helm with a worried look on his face. The students made fun of him. One of the students said, "We aren't afraid. Why should you be afraid?"

The captain looked at them and said, "Yes, you are too ignorant to be afraid."

Well, the disciples of Jesus were not too ignorant to be afraid. They had seen the storms on the Sea of Galilee, they were fishermen, they knew when to be afraid—and this was a time to be afraid.

In his first inaugural address, on March 4, 1933, Franklin Delano Roosevelt said that the only thing we had to fear was fear itself. That sounded nice; it was good rhetoric; it had a nice ring. The problem is that it wasn't true then and it isn't true now. We have a lot to fear, and there is something warped about the person who never experiences fear.

One of the most dangerous thoughts a Christian can have is to think a bold Christian has no fear, and then to deny the reality of that fear. I visit a lot of hospitals, and I will often ask a person who is facing surgery, "Are you frightened?" I get a great variety of answers to that question. Some Christians say, "No, Pastor, I'm not afraid. Christ is with me, and He has taken the fear." Others will say, "How can I be afraid? I'm a Christian."

Not too long ago, I was visiting a delightful lady in our church, and I asked her the question. Her answer was disarming in its honesty. She said, "Don't be silly! Of course I'm afraid. Do you think I'm a nut? People die in this place, so you pray for me." That was refreshing!

There is nothing Christian about the denial of reality. The courage of the Christian doesn't come without fear. When you don't have any fear, you don't need any courage. Courage can only be defined in the context of fear. If you never know fear, you will never know courage. The bold Christian ought to be the most realistic of people. Others live fairy tales, but not Christians. Pollyanna is another name for pagan. It ought to be quite different for Christians.

The Disciples' Mistakes

The disciples were afraid, and they had every reason to be afraid. Their fear was real and legitimate. However, they made some mistakes. We make them too.

Failure to Note the Peace of Jesus

First, the disciples made the mistake of failing to note the peace of Jesus. "And a great windstorm arose, and the waves beat into the boat, so that it was already filling. But He was in the stern, asleep on a pillow" (vv. 37–38a).

I have a friend who sometimes flies me around in his airplane. Flying in airplanes is not my favorite activity, but I don't mind flying with my friend. Do you know why? Because I can watch my friend's face. When he starts perspiring, I know it's time for me to commence praying. If he's calm, I'm calm, and if he's frightened, I'm frightened. In other words, I get my cue from the pilot, who knows when it is time to be afraid. If he isn't afraid, I figure I don't have to be either.

If I had been on the boat with Jesus, I believe I would have watched Him. I probably would have made several trips to the stern of the boat, and each time I would have checked on Jesus. As long as He was asleep my fear would be controllable. If Jesus had awakened, however, I would have gone into a panic.

There is a couple in our church who have been threatened with death if they didn't give in to certain demands. They have stood their ground, and sometimes it has been scary. The wife has been remarkably calm during the whole experience. I called them the other night after one particularly harsh threat and talked to her. She said, "Pastor, up until now I have been okay. But Ron was a little frightened tonight. When he gets frightened, I know it is time for me to be frightened."

Let me tell you something, when Jesus gets frightened, I know it is time to be frightened. But so far, when I have gone to Him, He has never been frightened.

Thomas Kelley talked about a calm altar in our heart where we can go to worship at any time. He said that no matter what is going on outside, we can go to that altar. What I am advocating is that we spend more time at the altar. Please understand that I am not giving the banal advice that if you are afraid, pray about it. What I am saying is that there is a calm place before the throne of Christ. We ought to be spending more time there, because we will always leave the calmness of His presence more calm than when we went in.

Most of my Christian life I have been a Christian simply because the Christian faith is true. I had determined intellectually that it was true, and if it was true, then, insofar as possible, I would live out its implications. That sounds good, but after a few years it gets sort of old. Understand that I am not talking about salvation. I was saved; I simply knew it more in my mind than I felt it in my heart.

About three years ago I prayed a life-changing prayer. I said, "Father, You know that I know a lot about You. I have a big library, I study the Bible, and I know theology. You also know that I'm never going to leave. No matter what happens, I am still going to keep on trucking. But, Father, I want to do more than just know *about* You. I want to know You. I want to experience Your presence in the way that a lot of my brothers and sisters experience it. I want the experience as well as the knowledge. Whatever it takes, allow me to know You the way they do."

I wouldn't try to tell you that I have since become a spiritual giant. I haven't. I don't even know enough to talk much about it, and I certainly haven't experienced it enough to teach about it. But over the past three years I have discovered God in a very significant and different way from the way I had known Him before. But, and here is the point, I have met God on the other side of silence. In the quiet, sometimes He comes. When my heart is still and waiting, sometimes I am able to hear the "soft sound of sandaled feet." Sometimes (not all the time) I can grow quiet and I am in His presence. On those occasions my fear is less, my heart is calmer, and my courage is greater. In fact, even the thought of those times calms my fears.

Failure to Note the Presence of Jesus

The disciples made another mistake. They failed not only to note the peace of Jesus, but they also failed to note the presence of Jesus. Paul wrote to the Romans:

NO MORE MR. NICE GUY!

> Who shall separate us from the love of Christ? Shall tribulation, or distress, or persecution, or famine, or nakedness, or peril, or sword? As it is written: "For Your sake we are killed all day long; We are accounted as sheep for the slaughter." Yet in all these things we are more than conquerors through Him who loved us. For I am persuaded that neither death nor life, nor angels nor principalities nor powers, nor things present nor things to come, nor height nor depth, nor any other created thing, shall be able to separate us from the love of God which is in Christ Jesus our Lord (Rom. 8:35–39).

Now that is a wonderful statement! It means that no matter what happens, a believer is never separated from Christ. Chuck Colson tells how Henry Kissinger disliked flying—except when Richard Nixon was on the airplane. When the president of the United States was on the plane, Kissinger was calm. Well, I'm not sure that would make me calm, but I'll tell you what does: the fact that Christ is present in my life, which means I don't have to face any difficulty or any fear by myself.

Failure to Note the Power of Jesus

That brings me to the third mistake the disciples made. Not only did they fail to note the peace and presence of Jesus, but they further failed to note the power of Jesus. "Then He arose and rebuked the wind, and said to the sea, 'Peace, be still!' And the wind ceased and there was a great calm" (v. 39). In the Greek language in which the New Testament was originally written, the command of Jesus to the wind is much stronger than can be reflected in the English translation. It would be closer if it were translated that Jesus said to the wind, "Will you shut up!" But that isn't the really amazing part—the amazing part is that the wind shut up.

The disciples really should not have been surprised that the wind obeyed Jesus. After all, they had heard the "clank" of the blind beggars' cups hitting the rocks by the side of the road; they had seen the crutches of the cripples thrown in the air; they had seen the dead walking and the lepers cleansed. Should it have been a surprise that Jesus had the power to speak to the wind? Of course not—but it was.

One of the spiritual exercises I have found helpful is the keeping of a spiritual diary. In the diary I record the times when God has been faithful. When I read the diary, I can find those places where I was scared to death, and where God was faithful. I am careful to record those experiences so that the next time I am frightened, I can go back and read the past and say, "If God didn't fail then, He won't fail now." (Or as my friend Ken Nanfelt said to me once, "Steve, if God is going to fail someone, it won't be you. If He fails someone He will start with Billy Graham or the Pope. You are just a peon.")

The power of Christ is so great that there is nothing outside His control. He is the King, and because He is the King I can know that if things fall apart, it is okay. I don't have to be afraid (or at least as afraid as I am), because He has written the play and He is the director, and He knows what He is doing.

There is a great comedy record featuring Mel Brooks as a very old man whose life is measured in thousands of years. The interviewer asks the old man if he was there when people started talking about God. He replied that he was there, and not only that, but God's name was Phil. He said that this guy by the name of Phil went out into the fields and said that he was God. A lot of people followed him. And then one day a lightning bolt came down and killed Phil. Brooks went on to say that the man who was standing next to Phil said, "There's somebody bigger than Phil!" Well, there is somebody bigger than Phil. Christians who are facing fear need to remember that.

HOW TO HANDLE FEAR

Now, the question before the house is this: If we are aware of the peace, the presence, and the power of Christ in our lives, what are the implications of that knowledge? In other words, when you are still afraid after realizing the peace, the presence, and the power of Christ, what do you do with your fear? I don't have a system, but I do have some helpful suggestions.

Define Your Fear

First, it is important for Christians to define their fear. There is nothing worse than being afraid and not knowing why. What is it that makes you afraid? Are you afraid people won't accept you? Are you afraid of pain? Are you afraid of poverty? Are you afraid of death? Definition is a prerequisite to dealing with fear.

One of the problems with many of us is that we have become so accustomed to our life of fear that we don't know what it is we fear. A man told me once, "Steve, I'm afraid not to be afraid." If you can't make a list of what frightens you, you ought not to be afraid.

I have a lawyer friend who lived a life of fear. He was a former alcoholic who found out, when he quit drinking, why he was drinking in the first place. It was his fear. He would call me and list everything that made him want to go back to the bottle. He would say, "Pastor, what if I can't make enough money to feed my family? What if I fail in court? What if I get sick?"

Finally, after listening to my friend's fears on numerous occasions, I said to him, "Jack, let's try an experiment. I want you to write down the ten things that worry you most. I want you to bring that list of your ten greatest fears to me, and I am going to put that list away in my desk. Six months from now we are going to have lunch together, and we are going to open the envelope and see how many of those fears were realized."

Six months later he called and reminded me about the lunch. To be honest with you, I was worried about that lunch. What if all his fears had become reality? What if my experiment had failed? Nevertheless, we met for lunch and I gave him the envelope, which he opened. Do you know what? Not a single one of the things he had feared had happened!

In the process of defining your fear, it is important that you define the "bottom line" results if the fear becomes a reality. Jesus said,

> For which of you, intending to build a tower, does not sit down first and count the cost, whether he has enough to finish it—lest, after he has laid the

138

foundation, and is not able to finish it, all who see it begin to mock him. . . . Or what king, going to make war against another king, does not sit down first and consider whether he is able with ten thousand to meet him who comes against him with twenty thousand? Or else, while the other is still a great way off, he sends a delegation and asks conditions of peace (Luke 14:28–29, 31–32).

Most of the time, when we define our fear and the costs of the fear's becoming a reality, two things happen. First, we find that in defining the fear it is not as great as we first supposed. And second, when we count the cost we find that while we would not like to pay the cost, if worse came to worse, we could handle it.

Confess Your Fear

After you define your fear, confess it. Confession is good for the soul, and it is good for boldness too. Honestly bring your fear before God. Tell Him that you are frightened and that you aren't sure you can act because of your fear.

Something I have discovered about boldness is that the Christian's lack of it is always on the "inside" and never perceived on the "outside." In other words, nobody but you and those you choose to tell know you are afraid. Make sure that one of the people you tell is God. The psalmist discovered a great truth: "I sought the LORD, and He heard me, and delivered me from all my fears" (Ps. 34:4).

Fear God Enough

Third, make sure you fear God enough. "Wait!" you say. "We aren't supposed to fear God, we are supposed to love Him." Yes, we are supposed to love God, but if you don't find yourself fearing Him, you are probably worshiping an idol. If you have not stood before God and been afraid, you have not stood before God.

The psalmist said, "The fear of the LORD is the beginning of wisdom" (Ps. 111:10). The fear of the Lord is also the beginning of boldness. John Witherspoon said, "It is only the fear of God that can deliver us from the fear of man."

I am not naturally confrontational. In other words, I would rather switch than fight. I don't like disagreements in the church or anyplace else. Time after time I have faced tense and frightening situations in the church where I have had to struggle with my need to be loved and my fear of rejection. I have occasionally had to struggle with the issue of whether to say something in the pulpit that needed to be said even if it made people mad.

Given my personality, a betting man would wager that I would not be confrontational. But let me tell you something interesting. If you were to talk to those who know me, they would tell you that I *am* confrontational—sometimes to the point of being obnoxious. Over and over again I hear from people in the church and on the staff, "Don't get Steve angry. It's dangerous."

How have I been able to deal with my need to be loved? I have a need to be loved by the Father more than I have a need to be loved by people. How have I been able to deal with my fear of confrontation? I am more afraid of God than I am of anybody else. I have done it my way and I have done it God's way. God's way is better. I would much rather have people angry at me than to have God angry at me.

Do What You Fear

Finally, go do whatever you fear. There is an old English proverb that says, "Fear knocked at the door; faith answered; nobody was there."

I have a pastor friend who, like me, has difficulty in confronting. He asked if I would help him. Over the course of our many conversations he told me about a man in his church who had caused serious problems in the fellowship. He had not only intimidated the people in the church (and that was bad enough), but he had also intimidated the pastor (and that can destroy the church). The problem was that he gave a significant amount of money to the church, and many of his relatives were in positions of leadership in the church. My pastor friend said, "Steve, I don't know what I can do about him. It would divide the church if I should confront him."

I said, "Let me give you a speech that you should recite to him. Invite this man to your study and say, 'I have had it up to my ears with you. Before this meeting is over, one of us is going to resign.' Then tell him all the things he has been doing to hurt the church. Tell him, 'This is not your church or my church, this is God's church, and He will not allow you to act in this manner anymore.' Then tell him that you are God's agent to make sure that he doesn't."

My pastor friend turned pale just thinking about it. But the problem was so big that he was willing to do anything. Two days later, my pastor friend called and said, "Steve, you wouldn't believe what has happened. The church member who has been giving the church all the trouble asked if I would forgive him. He said that he knew he had a problem and asked for my help. Not only that, he said that if I would give him another chance he would be different. Not only that, his two brothers came in and thanked me for what I did, and said that I was the first pastor in twenty years who had had the courage to do what needed doing."

Jesus said that Satan is the father of lies. His "whoppers" are often about what will happen if we stand. Most of the time we don't find out how big the lie is because we are not willing to call his bluff. But when you do, the joy of seeing God work in "cleaning up the mess" is one of the great gifts the Father gives to His own.

The point of all the above is this: It's okay to be afraid. It's just not okay to quit.

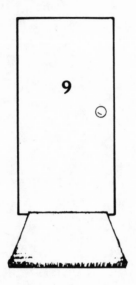

"For I say, through the grace given to me, to everyone who is among you, not to think of himself more highly than he ought to think, but to think soberly, as God has dealt to each one a measure of faith."

ROMANS 12:3

Harry
and the
Humble Habit

9

Not too long ago, a friend of mine was attending a worship service where a young woman sang a solo. He felt that she was reasonably good and so decided to compliment her. After the service was over, he went to her and said, "I liked your solo this morning, and I wanted to thank you."

The young woman looked down at her feet and said, "I appreciate your telling me that, but it wasn't me; it was the Holy Spirit."

My friend thought about saying, but didn't, "I'm glad it was the Holy Spirit, but I heard the Holy Spirit do a lot better last week when I heard Sandi Patti sing."

The statement of the young lady who did a reasonably good job of singing is reflective of many of us and our attitude toward our service for Christ. We feel the desperate need to make ourselves something less than we are, because somehow we have accepted the idea that a Christian ought to be humble (which is true) and that humility is self-effacement (which it isn't).

Humble Harry is the problem, and you can find Humble Harry at almost any church. He makes statements like, "I am nothing. I am a worm. I am good for nothing except standing in the corner. I am the lowest of the low." He whines and grovels and wrings his hands. Whenever he is complimented, he is unable simply to say, "Thank you." Whenever he is criticized, he assumes that the criticism is right and proper. Whenever he is given a position of leadership, he talks about his unworthiness. In Harry's view, Christian boldness is impossible because it contradicts his definition of humility. His definition of humility is not biblical, but it's hard to tell Harry that. He takes great pride in his humility, and it's about all he's got. If Humble Harry doesn't do something about his humble habit, however, he is never going to be used by God.

What is humility? Can a Christian be bold and humble at the same time? Can a humble Christian have convictions and voice them? Is humility the death of the strong Christian? Those are some of the questions we'll deal with in this chapter.

WHAT REAL HUMILITY IS NOT

In Colossians Paul wrote, "Let no one defraud you of your reward, taking delight in *false humility,*" (Col. 2:18, italics mine). Paul then talked about the regulations others had tried to impose on the church at Colosse. And then, just to make sure they didn't miss it, he said, "These things indeed have an appearance of wisdom in self-imposed religion, *false humility,* and neglect of the body, but are of no value against the indulgence of the flesh" (Col. 2:23, italics mine).

So it is clear that there is a real humility the Christian is to cultivate and a false humility the Christian is to avoid. Before we examine what real humility is, let's talk about what real humility isn't.

Humility Is Not Dishonesty

First, real humility is not dishonesty. Paul said, "For I say, through the grace given to me, to everyone who is among you, not to think of himself more highly than he ought to think, but to think soberly, as God has dealt to each one a measure of faith" (Rom. 12:3).

When I was growing up, I lived across the street from a girl who was my age. She was a good little girl most of the time, and I was not so good most of the time. I tried to tell my parents that boys were different from girls and that girls were supposed to be better than boys, but my parents knew "sexism" when they saw it, and they knew it long before they ever heard the word. Regarding academic matters, she was the bane of a little boy's existence. She got high marks and I got low marks in school, and I could have dealt with that except that she lived across the street and that was like living next door to Einstein. The real problem was that whenever it was time to get report cards, she would always say, "I am really afraid because my grades are going to go down this time." I relaxed because at least her report card would not, for a change, be compared to mine.

And then when the report cards came out, she would act surprised that on her report card there was one "A" after another. The same line would be repeated after a test. "I did horrible on that test. I'll be lucky if I even passed it." Of course she always had a perfect score. I was not very smart, but after a while I realized what was happening. She was lying, or (speaking from my now older and wiser perspective) perhaps she had a bad self-image.

What was normal in a little girl, I suspect, becomes a con when it happens with a pool hustler who comes into town to "play a little pool." After the local "sharks" have sized him up as a less than average pool player, he beats them all. Only after they are putting their money on the table do they realize they have been "taken."

In the church, a lot of people have been "taken" by the false humility of members of the Body of Christ who are constantly talking about how terrible they are. If you can sing, say so. If you are good at administration, say so. If you are a competent teacher, say so. And when you have done something particularly good, say that too.

In the church I serve, we are involved in the dramatic arts. In fact, our sanctuary is a "theater in the round." Recently after a great production of *Fiddler on the Roof*, I complimented one of the members of the cast. She smiled and said, "I was rather good, wasn't I?" Pride? Not at all. It was simply an illustration of Romans 12:3.

R. C. Sproul told about the time his eighth-grade English teacher was returning a homework assignment. To R. C.'s surprise, she read his composition to the entire class and posted the paper on the bulletin board as an example for everyone. Beneath the grade she had written, "R. C., don't ever let anyone tell you that you can't write."

When R. C. was working on one of his books, his editor said to him, "You've never been through our copy-editing procedures. Don't be discouraged if they make numerous critical suggestions." When he got the manuscript back from the copy editor, he figured out by counting the number of corrections on the first ten pages and averaging it out for the whole manuscript that there were approximately *ten thousand* critical marks. He wrote, "That should be enough to convince the most recalcitrant egomaniac that he ought to give up. But there they were, the words of my teacher, 'Never let anyone tell you that you can't write.' And here I am again—writing my fool fingers off."[1]

That is, of course, an illustration of the power of encouragement, but it is more than that. R. C. knew he could write, and he didn't let anybody, even someone who made ten thousand critical remarks, stop him. That isn't pride. If you have ever read any of Dr. Sproul's books, you know that he can write, and if he should ever start saying that he couldn't write, it would be outright dishonesty.

Too often Christians have believed that if they ever think of themselves as anything higher than something between a paramecium or a plankton, they have not been humble. And so, rather than being honest about the gifts God has given them, they decide to lie. The problem is that if you keep telling yourself you are no good, you will begin to think you are no good. If you are continually thinking it is right and proper that you fail, you will fail more often. If you are always denying God's gifts to you, pretty soon you begin to lose those gifts.

Our family once owned a German Shepherd by the name of Barnabas. We kept Barnabas fenced in our back yard. The fence was not very high, and Barnabas just assumed that we wouldn't put him behind a fence that he could jump. So he didn't. Now Barnabas hated motorcycles, and whenever he got the chance, he would chase them. (I don't have the slightest idea what he would have done if he had ever caught one.) There was a young man in our church who was constantly taunting Barnabas, and to make matters worse, the young man rode a motorcycle. One day Barnabas got so angry at this young man that he jumped over the fence. Not only did he jump over the fence, but he cleared it by at least three feet.

Later on Barnabas and I were discussing the incident, and he said to me, "You know, Steve, I never knew I could jump that fence. Did you see me? I not only jumped it, I sailed over it. But I've been thinking about my new-found ability, and I have decided that I'm not going to jump the fence anymore because the other dogs in the neighborhood will think I'm being proud of my fence-jumping abilities. After all, I'm a Christian dog, and I need to be humble. In fact, I probably couldn't jump it again if I wanted to. It just happened that God gave me, that once, an extra burst of strength because, apparently, God didn't like that 'turkey' any more than I did. But from now on, no more fence jumping. Fence jumping is only for prideful dogs, and I am a Christian dog."

I tried to tell Barnabas that fence jumping was not the problem. I suggested that he ought to watch going after young men he didn't like, but that fence jumping was a talent he was good at and should not deny it. I told him he was not being humble but dishonest. He didn't listen, though. After all, you can't tell a dog much. As a matter of fact, I never saw him jump that fence again.

Humility Is Not an Inferiority Complex

Second, real humility is not an inferiority complex. The church is the only organization in the world that takes what is neurotic and calls it "spirituality." There are some people who are thought to be spiritually mature because they are exceedingly humble when, in fact, they are just neurotic.

In the book of Job, Satan was reporting to God, and God asked Satan, "Have you considered My servant Job, that there is none like him on the earth, a blameless and upright man, one who fears God and shuns evil?" (Job 1:8). And so, given God's opinion of Job, we are free to use Job as an example of godliness. Yet when he was taunted by his friends, Job said, "No doubt you are the people, and wisdom will die with you! But I have understanding as well as you; I *am not inferior to you*" (Job 12:2–3, italics mine).

I love the apostle Paul's statement about his standing in the church. He said, "For I consider that I am not at all inferior to the most eminent apostles" (2 Cor. 11:5). In other words, Paul was not suffering from an inferiority complex. He knew that God had given him a place among the apostles, and you didn't see Paul going off in a corner and whining about his inferiority.

Someone tells about a young man who went to a psychiatrist. The psychiatrist said to him, "Son, the reason you have an inferiority complex is that you are inferior." When one is inferior and feels inferior, that is not neurotic, it is a simple recognition of reality. However, when one is not inferior and still feels inferior, that is not only neurotic, but it is also beneath any Christian.

Muretus, the poor scholar, was once found sick and dying by the side of the road. He was taken to the hospital, and two doctors, thinking Muretus was unconscious, stood beside his bed discussing the case. Just in case Muretus was conscious, however, they spoke in Latin so he wouldn't understand. One doctor said to the other, "Should we perform the operation on this poor, worthless creature?"

Muretus heard the comment, and raising himself up on his bed, he answered in perfect Latin: "Wilt thou call him worthless for whom Christ died?"

That's the point, isn't it? Our self-worth doesn't come from who we are, it comes from *Whose* we are. If Christ was willing to die for us, that makes us valuable.

Humility Is Not a Denial of Grace

Third, humility is not a denial of God's grace. Paul said, "But by the grace of God I am what I am, and His grace toward me was not in vain; but I labored more abundantly than they all, yet not I, but the grace of God which was with me" (1 Cor. 15:10).

The Bible teaches that God not only grants the believer salvation because of the death of Christ, but God also gives each Christian grace—gifts that are to be used in the church. After describing the working of God's Spirit in the believer, Paul said, "But one and the same Spirit works all these things, *distributing to each one* individually as He wills" (1 Cor. 12:11, italics mine). In other words, every believer is given a gift of God's grace that can be used to build up the Body of Christ. No person is without a significant part in the work of the church.

And yet even after many believers know clearly what the Bible teaches, they feel they are not capable of serving Him. They sit on the sidelines thinking that Christ has saved them but that, given their great sin, ignorance, clumsiness, or lack of training, they simply can't hope for any more than salvation. Ladies and gentlemen, that is not humility. That is a lie; and Satan has used it to emasculate countless Christians.

If you are a Christian, you have a place in God's economy. God has promised that He will give you a gift and what it takes to use it. I have a friend who was an executive in a large corporation. The business was bought by a different corporation, and my friend was no longer needed. He did, however, have a hard and fast contract that prevented the new management from firing him. Because they couldn't fire him but wanted him out, they simply stopped giving him anything to do. He would come to work and there would be no work. So he sat at his desk day after day reading the paper, doing the crossword puzzles, or sleeping. The whole situation became a contest between the business and my friend to see which one could hold out the longest.

A lot of Christians are that way. They have a contract without a connection. They just sit around trying to kill time until it is time to go home. That is not humility. It is a denial of God's grace.

And so there is a false humility. Fénelon (a seventeenth-century contemplative) wrote:

> There are plenty of people who practice sincere humility, and who, how-
> ever, are very far from that humility of heart of which I have just spoken, for
> outer humility, and one which has not its source in pure charity [i.e., love], is
> false humility. The more we think we are lowering ourselves, the more we are
> persuaded of our elevation. He who is conscious of lowering himself is not yet
> in his place.[2]

True Humility

I move the previous question: What is humility? Humility is simply knowing who you are in relation to your knowledge of who God is. In other words, it is knowing the truth about yourself in relation to the truth you know about God. Someone has said that humility is seeing yourself the way God sees you and acting accordingly.

A. W. Tozer talked of selling out to God. He wrote:

> Let no one imagine that he will lose anything of human dignity by this
> voluntary sell-out of his all to his God. He does not by this degrade himself as
> a man; rather he finds his right place of high honor as one made in the image
> of his Creator. His deep disgrace lay in his moral derangement, his unnatural

usurpation of the place of God. His honor will be proved by restoring again that stolen throne. In exalting God over all he finds his own highest honor upheld.[3]

You will say to me, "But we are sinners. The Bible says that the heart is deceitful above all things, and that means we are worms. Any time we say we are more than worms, are we not acting in a prideful manner?" No. No. No.

In John White's good book on depression, *The Masks of Melancholy,* he talked about the different models of depression. One of the models is the psychoanalytical model. Bibring, an early proponent of this model, saw depression as an ego state divorced from aggressive drives. (In plain English, that means that people who like being wimps get depressed.) Said White of Bibring:

> He suggested that helplessness was the critical factor in depression, help-lessness to achieve one's goals. To express the matter in analytic terms, the ego (the conscious, decision-making part of us) suffers a narcissistic injury and collapses when it perceives that its ideals (ego ideals) are unattainable. An ego ideal might be anything, a wish to be loved or to be "good" (holy) or to be secure or strong or kind or whatever.
>
> In simple terms we lose self-esteem when we fail to meet our own view of what is good and right. We are discouraged on perceiving the appalling gap between what we want to be and what we are, between our goals and our ability to perform. Christians will readily understand the dilemma. "Oh, wretched persons that we are! Who shall deliver us from this body of death?"[4]

That question of Paul's ("O wretched man that I am! Who will deliver me from this body of death?" Rom. 7:24) is a "before" question, and the "after" answer is one with tremendous power: "I thank God—through Jesus Christ our Lord! . . . There is therefore now no condemnation to those who are in Christ Jesus, who do not walk according to the flesh, but according to the Spirit" (Rom. 7:25–8:1). The "wretched man" is what Paul was *before* he met Christ, not after. When we continue to see ourselves as "wretched" after our encounter with Christ, we have missed the whole point.

What is the point? The point is that you are a sinner saved by grace, that you are now a child of God, that you are now in a proper relationship with God, that you are a creature and He is Creator, that you are a subject and He is the King, that you are a servant and He is the Master. When all of that is recognized and lived, you file it under humility.

So, you see, being humble is simply knowing who you are. A truly humble person is secure in that self-knowledge, and being secure in that knowledge, the Christian will sometimes offend. Sometimes the Christian will proclaim truth even if he or she might seem arrogant. But above all, the Christian will love with the love of Christ because only the truly humble person is able to truly love others. In order to love others, you have to get outside yourself. A humble person isn't one who thinks of himself or herself as less than he or she is. A truly humble person doesn't think about self at all.

Golda Meir, speaking to someone who was "groveling" in false humility, said, "Quit trying to be so humble. You're not that great." A Christian knows that. But while we aren't that great, Jesus is. He is our brother, and that gives us some great family connections.

In Tom Skinner's first book, *Black and Free*, he said something that every Christian ought to be able to say:

> I don't have to go out and struggle for human dignity anymore. Christ has given me true dignity. I don't have to go out and fight for human rights anymore because I have my rights. You see, I am a son of God. Jesus Christ is living in me and by virtue of the fact that I have received Jesus Christ into my life, the Bible says I have been given the authority to be a son of God. As a son of God, I have all the rights and privileges that go with that rank. I have the dignity that goes with being a member of the royal family of God. . . .
>
> In other words, my message to society is very simple. If you want status, maybe you ought to rub shoulders with me because I've got it as a son of God.[5]

Harry, you've got to do something about that humble habit. It makes you look silly. Not only that, it hurts the rest of us. You've given the impression that Christians can't do anything but put themselves down. As unfortunate as that is, there is something worse. We are the only Bible a lot of folks will ever read, and, like it or not, when people think of us they think of the God we worship.

For God's sake, hold your head up, and look me in the eye. Otherwise, people will think you are the child of a pauper.

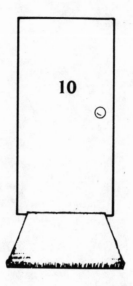

10

" 'Be angry, and do not sin': do not let the sun go down on your wrath, nor give place to the devil."

EPHESIANS 4:26–27

The Lamb
That
Roared

10

A Christian should never get angry. Right? Wrong! As a matter of fact, most Christians ought to get more angry than they do. Not only would it be good for them emotionally, but it would also be good for them spiritually.

I heard recently about a pastor who had a bad temper. He had done everything he could to restrain himself, but the people in the church had learned not to push him too far. One day some people in the church caused a serious problem, and it almost divided the church. The pastor was in his study fuming and pacing when his associate came in. The young associate said, "Pastor, I know you are upset, but try to restrain your anger."

"Young man," the pastor said as he turned to his associate, "don't tell me to restrain my anger! You are now seeing more restrained anger than you will ever see in your lifetime!"

God knows there are plenty of reasons for anger. The long lines at the pornography stores and the abortion clinics make the Disney World lines look small. Child pornography, violence, and perversion run rampant, and if the Christian community expresses any concern at all the world yells "censorship" and "freedom of the press." Doesn't it make you angry?

The news and entertainment media in this country feel free to make fun of the sacred with impunity. God has become the subject matter for jokes. The church is seen as the dying last bastion for Neanderthals. All Christians are somehow portrayed as shallow and superficial spoilsports out to stop anybody who wants to have a bit of innocent fun. Doesn't it make you angry?

A prominent senator told the Christian community that they ought to stick to their prayers. The slogan for freedom of speech has been changed and hardly anybody notices. It now reads: "I may not agree with what you say, but I will defend with my life your freedom to say it—as long as you're not a Christian." In other words, anybody can say anything no matter how silly and banal as long as the person talking isn't a Christian. Doesn't it make you angry?

The poor go hungry and the politicians keep buying their votes with empty promises. A group of entertainers sing a song to raise a mere pittance for hunger (compared to the millions and millions given to the poor by Christians), and one would think the "second coming" had arrived, judging from the attention the media give them. Meanwhile, a child living in the slums who can't read and who doesn't have enough to eat wonders why things are so bad. Doesn't it make you angry?

The religious manipulators keep pushing their products and selling their God-blessed success. Down in the marketplace you can hear the harsh bark of the con men, you can handle the bright wares of the peddlers, you can laugh at the false faces of the actors, and it's hard to tell which are the Christians without a scorecard. Doesn't it make you angry?

In the schools, parents are told to shut up, pay their taxes, and leave the education of their children to the experts. After all, what do parents know about education? If the books teach an amoral system of irrelevant platitudes; if the teachers think truth is decided by a vote; if the administrators, without blushing, will talk about academic freedom in the teaching of alternate sexual lifestyles, political witchcraft, psychological nonsense, and sociological hocus-pocus but draw the line with any mention of God; what is that to parents? Doesn't it make you angry?

On the home front, families are falling apart, divorce is rampant, venereal disease is increasing at an alarming rate, and the Neros of the pagan world keep playing their violins. In international relations, there is the increasing possibility that someone will pull the trigger on a real shooting match. Nations fall to the voracious appetite of the hungry bear, and the Chamberlains of the world keep twirling their umbrellas. Doesn't it make you angry?

There is a lot to make a Christian angry. If that is so, why aren't we angry? It may be because we have not understood what the Bible says about anger. It may be because we have not really faced the issues. It may be because we are afraid of anger and would rather keep the waters calm no matter the cost. And then it may be that we think lack of anger is a Christian virtue. Whatever the reason, more Christians ought to be angry. The fact that we aren't, I believe, is a significant problem. Let's talk about it.

ANGER IN THE BIBLE

If you take the time to read the Bible, you will see men and women who were loving, committed, and faithful, but you will also see men and women who were angry. From Genesis to Revelation, one finds men and women who had their calm waters disturbed by God's Spirit, and who reacted with a righteous anger that caused change. If you ever think there is something ungodly about anger, you ought to read the prophets or listen to Paul.

The Bible says, "He who is slow to anger is better than the mighty" (Prov. 16:32). Please note that word *slow*. If God had wanted to say "never," He would have said "never." Again in the book of Proverbs we read, "The discretion of a man makes him slow to anger" (Prov. 19:11). Please note again the word *slow*. Jesus said, "But I say to you that whoever is angry with his brother without a cause shall be in danger of the judgment." If Jesus had meant to leave out the phrase "without a cause," He would have left it out. In Ephesians 4:26 we read, "'Be angry, and do not sin': do not let the sun go down on your wrath." If getting angry were, in itself, a sin, God would have said, "Don't be angry." But He didn't say that simply because He didn't *want* to say it.

Aristotle said, "Anybody can become angry. That is easy, but to be angry with the right person, and to the right degree, and at the right time, and for the right purpose, and in the right way, that is not within everybody's power." He was right, and to find out the right person, the right degree, and the right time isn't always easy. There does seem to be a contradiction in the Scripture. For instance, in Ephesians 4:31 Paul seems to contradict what he said just a few verses earlier. He said, "Let all bitterness, wrath, anger, clamor, and evil speaking be put away from you." The contradiction is, however, apparent and not real. What Paul in particular and the Bible in general teach is that certain kinds of anger are appropriate and certain other kinds of anger are not appropriate.

JESUS' ANGER

If you want to know when anger is appropriate, the best thing to do is to find a model. The best model is always Jesus. Let's look at His anger. You will find the incident in John 2:13–25:

Now the Passover of the Jews was at hand, and Jesus went up to Jerusalem. And He found in the temple those who sold oxen and sheep and doves, and the moneychangers doing business. When He had made a whip of cords, He drove them all out of the temple, with the sheep and the oxen, and poured out the changers' money and overturned the tables. And He said to those who sold doves, "Take these things away! Do not make My Father's house a house of merchandise!" Then His disciples remembered that it was written, "Zeal for Your house has eaten Me up." So the Jews answered and said to Him, "What sign do You show to us, since You do these things?" Jesus answered and said to them, "Destroy this temple, and in three days I will raise it up." Then the Jews said, "It has taken forty-six years to build this temple, and will You raise it up in three days?" But He was speaking of the temple of His body. Therefore, when He had risen from the dead, His disciples remembered that He had said this to them; and they believed the Scripture and the word which Jesus had said.

Now when He was in Jerusalem at the Passover, during the feast, many believed in His name when they saw the signs which He did. But Jesus did not commit Himself to them, because He knew all men, and had no need that anyone should testify of man, for He knew what was in man.

In order to understand the anger of Jesus in this particular situation, one must understand a little of the context. During the feast of Passover, all Jews within a twenty-mile radius were expected to be in Jerusalem. Further, Jews all over the world flowed into the holy city to celebrate Passover so that sometimes there were as many as two hundred fifty thousand people there for the feast.

Almost all of my ministry I have been a pastor in vacation areas, and during that time I have learned a principle: Wherever there are tourists, there will be people around to fleece the tourists. During the Passover, Jerusalem was no exception. What was unusual in Jerusalem was that the main fleecing place was the temple.

Passover required that every family make an animal sacrifice. The sacrifice couldn't be just any sacrifice; it had to be a sacrifice "without blemish." A sacrificial animal could be purchased almost anywhere in Jerusalem at a reasonable price. The problem with that, however, was that the temple inspectors (who approved the sacrifices) had worked a deal with those who sold sacrificial animals in the temple at a 40 percent mark-up. Then the "kickback" went to the inspector. You can bet your last dollar that unless you purchased your sacrificial animal in the temple, you weren't going to get it by the temple inspectors.

But that isn't all. There was a temple tax. Now, that isn't bad in itself. After all, there are expenses in running any institution, even religious institutions. The problem was that the tax could not be paid in foreign currency. The money changers provided the exchange from the dirty money of the other countries into the clean money of the temple—and they did it at a healthy profit to themselves.

When Grassus conquered Jerusalem and raided the treasury (54 B.C.), he took out of the treasury some four million dollars. I would suggest that that kind of money is enough to tempt a preacher to put his hand in the collection plate. And so, I would further suggest, the religious leaders were ironically and sinfully "obeying" the Scripture in their actions in Jerusalem: "He was a stranger and I took him in" (Matt. 25:43, paraphrase).

At any rate, it was the above kind of action, directed against the poor, that made Jesus angry. Let's examine His anger.

His Anger Was Restrained

First, please note that the anger of Jesus was restrained. I get angry easily. A few years ago, a woman in our congregation brought her brother, a psychiatrist, to one of our worship services. When it was over, she asked her brother what he thought of me. His comment was more revealing than I like to admit. He said, "I don't think I have ever seen anyone living so close to the edge of hostility."

When I get convicted about my anger, as with my other sins, I go to the Gospels to try to justify it. Sometimes I find myself pointing to the Scripture we are considering and saying, "See there, your anger isn't so bad. Jesus was angry too." But the problem is that it simply won't wash. When I go to the Gospels honestly, it is very hard to think of Jesus as an angry man. I find that I have no trouble in thinking of Jesus as strong, loving, compassionate, and wise, but I have great difficulty in thinking of Him as angry.

When I was in seminary, it was popular to think of Jesus as a political revolutionary. We went to great lengths to prove that if Jesus' incarnation had taken place in the twentieth century, He would have been involved in liberal and even socialist political activities. But we were kidding ourselves. Jesus was not a political revolutionary, and He was not an angry man. Jesus said, "Come to Me, all you who labor and are heavy laden, and I will give you rest. Take My yoke upon you and learn from Me, for I am gentle and lowly in heart, and you will find rest for your souls" (Matt. 11:28–29).

While Jesus got angry, His anger was restrained. He had plenty about which to be angry. There was the frustration of not being understood. There was the dullness of His disciples. When He was in trouble, all His disciples fled and one of His closest followers denied Him. He came to serve, and He found His followers arguing about who would be the greatest in the kingdom. He encountered indifference, rebellion, and unbelief—and yet He can't be thought of as an angry man.

If I am going to use Jesus as my model, I will sometimes get angry. But if my friends think of me as an angry person or if I am angry most of the time, I've missed it.

His Anger Was Selfless

Second, Jesus' anger was not only restrained, but it was also selfless. Please note in the incident under consideration that Jesus was not angry because He didn't get what was coming to Him. He was not angry because somebody had crossed Him. He was not angry because somebody had not been nice to Him or because someone had failed to speak to Him. Rather, He was angry because others had been hurt. He was angry because the temple of God had been used to oppress the poor. And He was angry because His Father was being dishonored.

I don't know about you, but I am usually angry when my ego has been damaged. Not only that, I make up little conversations where I, of course, make my point with devastating accuracy. I think, I *know what he is going to say. He is going to tell me that I am a dictator in the church, and how can I expect anything to happen here if I am making all the decisions. Then I will tell him that if I didn't make the decisions, they wouldn't get made, and that I haven't seen him beating down the door to help. I will tell him that when he has earned the right to be heard, I will listen to him. Then he will tell me where to go, and I will respond that I have already been there and he has been a part of it. Then he will see the error of his ways and apologize for what he has said.*

It never works out that way, of course. The person I have created in my mind doesn't exist. I "got" the "straw man" in my mind, but the real person, I always find out, is someone who has dreamed conversations in his mind where he "gets" me. The anger that is finally expressed (if it ever is) usually creates more anger and broken relationships. If the anger is never expressed, the result is the same.

Jesus' anger was never ego-centered, and ours almost always is. Therein lies the problem. If I could ever work up my anger over someone else's hurt or rejection, I would be able to be more like Jesus.

When the prophets cried out against injustice, they did it for two reasons. First, God told them to speak, and second, they were angry about a situation that hurt people.

I am not saying that there is no legitimate anger when one is personally involved. However, I am saying that if most of our anger is because we have been hurt, crossed, or ignored, it is not the kind of anger Jesus expressed. He ought to have been angry at His betrayal; He ought to have been angry at His trial; He ought to have been angry while He was hanging on the cross. And yet He was not angry in those places, only hurt. That says a lot about the concern of a man. His concern was for others, and His anger reflected that concern.

When James Calvert went out to Fiji in 1838, he was told by the captain of the ship on which he sailed that he was going to a land of cannibals. The captain tried to dissuade Calvert from going by saying, "You are risking your life and all those with you if you go among such savages. You will all die."

Calvert replied, "We died before we came here."

Paul said, "For the death that He [Jesus] died, He died to sin once for all; but the life that He lives, He lives to God. Likewise you also, reckon yourselves to be dead indeed to sin, but alive to God in Christ Jesus our Lord" (Rom. 6:10–11). Appropriating the reality of Christ's death in our lives is a lifelong process, but insofar as we have died to self, our anger will be pure and proper.

His Anger Was Righteous

Third, note that the anger of Jesus was also righteous. In other words, Jesus' anger could be described as "righteous indignation" because it was directed at people who had violated the clear standards of Scripture. Out of Jesus' righteousness, He became angry.

"Righteous indignation," said a little boy, "is when you get angry without cussing." There may be something to that, but sometimes one even uses strong language to express the anger of God toward a particular situation.

I was speaking at a "Christian" college not too long ago and was asked by the chaplain if it would be all right for him to set up some counseling appointments with me for some of the students. I agreed, and the college put me in a small office with some secretarial help to keep the appointments lined up properly. I sat down behind the desk expecting to encounter the common problems of students. I suspected there would be questions about sexuality, suicide, and relationships. I was surprised, however, when instead student after student told me how their faith had been weakened and sometimes destroyed by one professor on campus. The more I listened, the angrier I became.

At the end of the day, I was fuming and ready to go after this particular professor. And then I realized the damage I was going to cause if I didn't control and direct my anger. I asked God to forgive me for the anger, and in my spirit I heard Him say, "Son, there is nothing to forgive. I'm more angry than you are. Control it—but use it." I did, and the professor is no longer teaching at that college.

Dr. Donald Grey Barnhouse, a former pastor of Tenth Presbyterian Church in Philadelphia, offered a question and answer session on most Wednesday evenings. One evening a woman raised her hand and said, "Dr. Barnhouse, I attend a church where the pastor doesn't believe in the Virgin Birth or the Resurrection. He makes fun of the Bible and takes great delight in showing us contradictions in the Bible. What should I do?"

Those who were there said that Dr. Barnhouse took off his glasses and in total seriousness said, "Madam, you should pray that he die."

Improper anger? No, I don't think so. I think he was expressing God's anger, and sometimes God gets very angry. I have often prayed, "Father, teach me to weep where You weep, to love what You love, and to be angry where You are angry."

One of the interesting books of the Bible is the book of Esther, and one of the interesting things about that book is that the name of God is never mentioned. The book of Esther tells the story of how wicked Haman plotted to kill all the Jews in the Persian Empire. The story ends with Esther and the Jews saved and Haman being hanged on his own gallows.

Out of the story of Esther has come the Jewish Feast of Purim. Purim is a peculiar feast because it does not require fasting or religious services, nor was there any prohibition of labor. During Purim there is great joy and happiness. When the book of Esther is read, the reaction of the Jews (particularly when they were being persecuted) is one of verbal cursing and expressions of anger whenever the name Haman is read, and joy and blessing when the name of Esther is read.

What nonsense. Right? Wrong. God has provided a festival for the Jews to express their anger. It was a proper anger that was psychologically healthy because it was an anger against injustice, persecution, and oppression. God was angry and therefore gave His people a feast in which they could express their anger.

Jesus' anger was righteous anger. He was angry where the Father was angry.

His Anger Was Controlled

Fourth, Jesus' anger was controlled. I once heard former Senator Walter Judd tell about the time Barry Goldwater was running for president. Goldwater, you will remember, was very clear about what he thought, and he didn't care where he said what he thought. He would come to Florida and speak against the excesses of Social Security, and he would go to Tennessee and speak against the Tennessee Valley Authority. One learned to respect his integrity if not his political acumen.

At any rate, Judd said that he went to Goldwater and said, "Barry, you have got to learn that sometimes it is best to be quiet. Every time you pass a bull in a field, you don't have to wave a red flag in his face."

Jesus would have agreed with Judd's advice. Jesus' anger was controlled. There was plenty of injustice to which Jesus never directed His anger; there were plenty of violations of God's law where Jesus could have expressed His anger, but didn't. He picked His time and His place.

One of the best sermons I ever preached was my first Easter sermon. I was a young pastor in a small church on Cape Cod. All winter long we had been trying to get people to the worship services of the church, and we had not been very successful. Then Easter came, and I looked out from the side door at all the pagans who had come to show off their Easter finery. As I stood by the door, something "snapped" in me, and I became so angry I was ready to scream.

I was in my study pacing back and forth and thinking about how I was going to get those turkeys. The janitor of the church heard the noise coming from my study and, without knocking, opened the door, walked in, and sat down. He watched me walk back and forth for a couple of minutes. And then he said, "Pastor, I know you are mad, and you probably have every reason to be mad. But you remember that you will only get one shot at most of those people out there. Don't blow it."

His words were like cold water. I didn't stop being angry, but I stopped and thought about it. Then I used my anger to speak clearly and strongly about God's action in raising Jesus from the dead. There was power in that sermon because it was the power of controlled anger.

When Jesus got angry, He took the time to braid a whip. If we would take the time to braid our whips, we would be more effective in our anger. Someone has said that anger is the wind that blows out the lamp of the mind. That is true, and if it is left unrestrained it is of no use whatsoever.

His Anger Was Effective

Finally, I want you to know that Jesus' anger was effective. Note that the religious leaders did not question the propriety of Jesus' actions. Rather, they asked Him if He had a sign to show that He had the authority to do what He did. It was that question that opened the door for a witness from Jesus that caused belief. John wrote, "Now when He was in Jerusalem at the Passover, during the feast, many believed in His name when they saw the signs which He did" (2:23).

One time I got very angry at an officer in a church I served. I was so angry, in fact, that I locked the door so he couldn't get out while I gave him a "piece of my mind." Do you know what that accomplished? Nothing. That officer never again darkened the door of our church or, for that matter, any other church. I have gone back to that man and asked for his forgiveness. He told me that he forgave me, but he still has not gone back to a church to this day.

So often my anger does nothing but hurt other people. Thank God, He isn't finished with me yet. I often pray, "Father, make my anger like the anger of Jesus. Make my anger a positive force for good. If it doesn't help, help me to be quiet."

One time the president of Czechoslovakia visited the Paris office of a news service. One of the correspondents noted that the president never became angry. The newsman commented on it and asked the reason.

The president replied, "I am a short man, and short men must never become angry. When a big man becomes enraged, it seems impressive, but when a little man gets angry and starts sputtering and fuming, he just looks silly."

Jesus was a very big man. His anger was impressive.

We must be careful, however, because we are very little. We ought to be angry, but we must be careful lest we appear only silly.

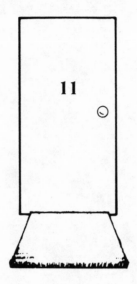

"Do not lie to one another, since you have put off the old man with his deeds."

COLOSSIANS 3:9

The Tyranny
of
Testimony

11

Manford Gutzke, who has for years taught the Bible over the radio, once told me about a small church in the town in Texas where he grew up. This particular church believed not only in baptismal regeneration (i.e., the belief that the sacrament of baptism saves you), but also in baptismal sanctification (i.e., the belief that the sacrament of baptism makes you perfect). These folks actually believed that once a Christian was baptized, thereafter there would be no sin in that person's life.

One winter, during a revival meeting, a man came forward and claimed Christ as his Savior. Having been taught the doctrines of this particular church, he insisted on being baptized. That would have been okay except that it was the middle of winter and the river was frozen over. The deacons of the church tried to talk him out of it, but the more they talked the more he insisted.

The next Sunday, a very cold day, the members of the church gathered by the river to baptize their new brother. A hole was cut through the ice, and one of the deacons went out into the river to help with the baptism. The man, according to plan, went under the water and came up shouting, "Hallelujah! It is wonderful to be saved and sanctified. It is so wonderful," he shouted, "I don't even feel the cold."

The old deacon who was assisting in the baptism stood behind him and began to speak through chattering teeth and blue lips, "We . . . we . . . we've got to do it again. He's lying!"

Wouldn't it be wonderful if there were some way to detect when people were lying in their testimony? Time after time I have heard brothers and sisters tell how God had changed them, healed them, and sanctified them. I used to have the suspicion that they were lying. Since becoming a pastor I am no longer suspicious—I know. A lot of the testimony we hear in the church is either a lie or has covered the truth so well that it is the same thing as a lie.

Don't get me wrong. I believe that when Christians have found victory in their lives they should give testimony to that fact. I believe we ought to praise God in the church for what He has done. The psalmist wrote, "Praise the Lord! I will praise the Lord with my whole heart, in the assembly of the upright and in the congregation. The works of the LORD are great" (Ps. 111:1–2a).

I believe in testimony, but I also believe that testimony should be honest. If it were more honest, it would be more helpful.

THE TYRANNY OF DISHONEST TESTIMONY

Have you ever considered the tyranny of the dishonest Christian testimony? It is a terrible problem because it robs Christians of their boldness. We begin to think that we must either be like some other Christian or, if we can't *be* like them, at least act like them. And the joke is that often the Christian we want to be like isn't like what we thought at all.

It reminds me of the old story of the folks at the phone company who set their clocks by the 12 o'clock whistle at the town factory. When the noon whistle would blow, the clock at the phone company would be set.

Every day the phone company would get a call from the same person asking the time. This went on for months until the operator asked, "Who are you? You call every day asking for the time, and I certainly don't mind because it is a part of my job, but you must have a horrible watch if it gets out of sync every day."

The man on the other end of the line replied, "I'm not calling to set my watch. I work at the factory, and so many people set their watches by our noon whistle that I call you every day to make sure it's blown at the proper time."

One of the problems in the church is that Christians often gauge their Christian life by others when those same people are gauging their Christian life by us. As a result, there is a lot of dishonesty and fear. We think, *If I should step out of line, others might think I'm not a Christian. If I should say something improper, my witness would come apart. If I should confess the way I really feel, the brothers and sisters would be shocked. If I should get honest, the church would excommunicate me.*

It's hard to be bold when you are constantly looking over your shoulder. It's hard to be bold when you live in the fear that someone will judge you if you are wrong. It is hard to speak boldly if you think others are weighing every word, checking every nuance, judging every thought. It's hard to be bold if you aren't free.

TYPES OF TESTIMONY THAT ARE LIES

There are five areas where Christians ought to be very careful when listening to another's testimony. If the testimony or witness that we encounter in any way denies humanness, covers sin, ignores process, universalizes experience, or lessens grace, that testimony is a lie. Does that surprise you? It shouldn't, but if it does you are probably trying to live up to somebody else's false standards, and you can't do that and be bold at the same time.

Testimony That Denies Humanness

First, disbelieve any testimony that denies humanness. The psalmist wrote, "As a father pities his children, so the LORD pities those who fear Him. For He knows our frame; He remembers that we are dust. As for man, his days are like grass; As a flower of the field, so he flourishes. For the wind passes over it, and it is gone, and its place remembers it no more" (Ps. 103:13–16). Matthew said that when Jesus saw the multitudes "He was moved with compassion for them, because they were weary and scattered, like sheep having no shepherd" (Matt. 9:36). He spoke to our weakness when He said, "Come to Me, all you who labor and are heavy laden, and I will give you rest. Take My yoke upon you and learn from Me, for I am gentle and lowly in heart, and you will find rest for your souls. For My yoke is easy and My burden is light" (Matt. 11:28–30).

I am often asked if I believe it is possible for Christians to have emotional and psychological problems. I am always surprised by the question, and I often respond, "Do you believe that if you stick a Christian with a pin he or she will bleed?" The questioner usually allows that Christians bleed just like everybody else. Then I say, "What makes you think that Christians' emotions don't bleed and get hurt too?"

Because the testimonies of many today teach it, we have accepted the notion that once one becomes a Christian, one is thereby protected from human weakness and failure. That comes from the pit of hell. No matter what anybody tells you, Christians are not exempt from anything pagans have to face, with the exception of hell. I am not sure it's biblical, but I think it's true that for every pagan who gets hurt, a Christian gets hurt; for every pagan who gets cancer, a Christian gets cancer; for every pagan who doubts, a Christian has doubts; for every pagan who has to go through emotional problems, a Christian has to go through emotional problems; and for every pagan who gets weary, depressed, and hurt, a Christian gets weary, depressed and hurt. Why? So the world can see the difference in how we respond! Paul said:

> But we have this treasure in earthen vessels, that the excellence of the power may be of God and not of us. We are hard pressed on every side, yet not crushed; we are perplexed, but not in despair; persecuted, but not forsaken; struck down, but not destroyed—always carrying about in the body the dying of the Lord Jesus, that the life of Jesus also may be manifested in our body (2 Cor. 4:7–10).

One of the reasons a lot of Christians never get bold is that they believe boldness is only for supersaints. One time my friend David O'Dowd was talking to a woman who was trying to escape her responsibility as a Christian. She said to him, "David, it's okay for you to talk like that. After all, you're a pastor."

"I'm not going to let you get away with that," David responded. "There is nothing magical in my ordination. When I was ordained, I did not thereby become exempt from fear and weakness, and any time you use my pastoral status to excuse yourself, you are rationalizing your refusal to stand."

If you are waiting until you are no longer human before you act, you will wait forever. Early in my ministry I was invited to be a part of an organization that was considered divisive in some circles. I didn't have anyone to talk to about what I should do, so I called the late Dr. Addison Leitch, who was then the academic dean at Gordon Seminary. He very graciously asked me to come to his study and talk. I don't remember all he said to me on that occasion, but I do remember that he said, "Steve, don't ever assume when you read church history that our heroes were not human. Calvin, Luther, and Melanchthon were just as afraid and confused as we are. They simply trusted God and did the best they could. You should do that too."

Now, before I go on to the next point, let me go down a small side-road. It is often our humanness, our weakness, and our suffering that are used by God for others. Paul wrote to the Colossians, "I now rejoice in my sufferings for you, and fill up in my flesh what is lacking in the afflictions of Christ, for the sake of His body, which is the church" (Col. 1:24). Paul was not saying that there is something lacking in the atonement of Christ for our salvation. He was simply saying that Jesus set a pattern of suffering, that suffering is allotted to the church until Christ returns, and that he (Paul) was suffering for them.

G. Campbell Morgan told of the time he was a pastor of a church in North London. He got very ill and was close to death. In addition to the horror of the illness, he was depressed and afflicted emotionally. He went to see Joseph Parker, the pastor of City Temple, and asked why he (Morgan) had to go through such a terrible experience. Parker said, "Son, never mind. Your people will get the value. There will come another note into your preaching which you never could have found if you had not suffered."

The point is this: It is often because of our weakness that we are able to help others. Charles Spurgeon, who was given to terrible periods of depression, told his students:

> Good men are promised tribulation in this world, and ministers may expect a larger share than others, that they may learn sympathy with the Lord's suffering people, and so may be fitting shepherds of an ailing flock. Disembodied spirits might have been sent to proclaim the word, but they could not have entered into the feelings of those who, being in this body, do groan, being burdened; angels might have been ordained evangelists, but their celestial attributes would have disqualified them from having compassion on the ignorant; men of marble might have been fashioned, but their impassive natures would have been a sarcasm upon our feebleness, and a mockery of our wants. Men, and men subject to human passions, the all-wise God has chosen to be his vessels of grace; hence these tears, hence these perplexities and castings down.[1]

Testimony That Covers Sin

Second, when you hear or see a testimony that seems to cover sin, stay away from it. It's a lie. The Bible says, "The heart is deceitful above all things, and desperately wicked; who can know it?" (Jer. 17:9). The Apostle John wrote, "If we say that we have no sin, we deceive ourselves, and the truth is not in us" (I John 1:8). Paul quoted from the Old Testament to confirm his own understanding of human nature: "There is none righteous, no, not one; there is none who understands; there is none who seeks after God. They have all gone out of the way; they have together become unprofitable; there is none who does good, no, not one" (Rom. 3:10–12).

I could quote more Scripture, of course, but you get the point. If someone gives you the impression that he has somehow risen above sin, he is either lying to himself or to you or both. A friend of mine compared two famous preachers this way: "Dr. Jones gives the impression when he is preaching that he is talking to everybody but himself. One feels that he has never sinned. On the other hand, Dr. Smith identifies with us. He has the same struggle with sin that we have." Thank God for honest Christians. They make us feel there is hope, and that God can even use a sinner.

I am not saying that Christians ought to bask in their sin, or be proud of it, or proclaim it on the rooftops, but I do believe Christians ought to be honest. (Someone tells of the priest who listened to the confession of one man for over an hour. He finally interrupted him and said, "Sir, you aren't confessing; you're bragging!") It is the only way other sinners will be encouraged to be bold. If anyone believes that he must be good enough to be bold enough to do any good, he will wait until glory. And if we, in our testimony, give the impression that only "good" people are of any use to God, those who know us will know we are hypocrites, and those who don't will give up, thinking it is impossible.

Testimony That Ignores the Process

Third, whenever you hear or see a testimony that ignores the process of sanctification, that suggests God always works by changing people overnight, stay away from it. When Paul wrote that we ought to "receive one who is weak in the faith," he taught, at minimum, that people are at different places in their Christian walk. C. S. Lewis said that if two people are converted to Christ at the same time, one should not expect that they turned around on the road at the same place. If you and I should become Christians at the same time, for instance, our experience with Christ would be different because we are different people.

Let's suppose (which I am sure is true) that you are a wonderful person who naturally likes people and enjoys helping others. Let's assume that before you became a Christian you visited the sick in hospitals, had compassion on the poor, and loved the downtrodden. On the other hand, let's suppose (which some people are sure is true) that I am a naturally mean person who is a Scrooge without the spirit. Let's suppose that before I became a Christian I didn't like children or cats.

Now, when we became Christians we were at different places on the road. Conversion means "to turn around," and when we turned around you were far ahead of me. Suppose that you continue to do what you have always done, and suppose that I continue to do what I have always done with two exceptions—I pet a kitten and smile at one little boy. If those things happen, it may be that God will be more pleased with me than with you. It may be, because I have to come so far, that God sees more progress in my walk of faith than in yours.

There are certain actions I excused when my children were small. After all, they were only children, and children have certain limitations. If my daughters didn't put everything away in its place, if they sometimes said dumb things, if they often tried and failed, that was all part of learning and growing. But my daughters are young women now, and they have put away childish actions. What I expected from them as children is far different from what I expect of them as adults.

I believe that the Father deals with His children in the same way. He recognizes that we are in the process of sanctification and that the process has different people at different places. He expects more from some than from others. James said, "My brethren, let not many of you become teachers, knowing that we shall receive a stricter judgment" (James 3:1). Jesus told a parable of the faithful steward in which He described two different kinds of stewards. He said, "And that servant who knew his master's will, and did not prepare himself or do according to his will, shall be beaten with many stripes. But he who did not know, yet committed things worthy of stripes, shall be beaten with few" (Luke 12:47–48a). When a testimony to God's action is given, it is important to remember the process.

Did you ever think that the great can be the enemy of the good? Too often young Christians listen to the testimony of "mature" Christians and think that God requires them to be at the same place and, at some point, will take them there instantly. They realize that hasn't happened to them, so they give up. It is hard to be bold if your model is perfect, instantly attained boldness.

Testimony That Universalizes Experience

Fourth, beware of a testimony that universalizes experience. In Luke 15, you will find the parable of the lost sheep. Jesus said, "What man of you, having a hundred sheep, if he loses one of them, does not leave the ninety-nine in the wilderness, and go after the one which is lost until he finds it?" (v. 4). Among other things, Jesus is saying in the parable that God knows us as individuals. If that is true, and it is, then He *treats* us as individuals.

I have always wanted to be an evangelist. Whenever I hear Billy Graham preach, I ask the Father about it. "Father, why can't I be like him? He is able to be on the cutting edge, to have the thrilling experience of seeing thousands come to know You. Why can't I be an evangelist too?"

The Father's answer is always the same: "You are not Billy Graham, and I will never judge you as Billy Graham. I will judge you as Steve

Brown. I have called you to be a pastor and a Bible teacher. Be what you are."

One of the problems with a testimony of experience (baptism of the Holy Spirit, a warm and fuzzy walk with Jesus, a high degree of spiritual power, a vision, a miracle, and so on) is that those who listen believe they ought to have the same experience—often because that's what the speaker tells them. But nothing could be further from the truth. It is important to remember that doctrine should be universalized and experience should be particularized. If we ever reverse that, Christians will think that unless they share the experience, they have no business in being a bold Christian.

Testimony That Denies God's Grace

Now, if you have read the above carefully, you're aware that there could be a problem. There's the danger of so expressing our humanness, confessing our sin, acknowledging the process, and particularizing our experience that a testimony becomes nothing more than a pile of negatives. But a testimony, when it is honest, is truthful about more than failure and humanness. It is also honest about success, growth, and victory. So I would add one more kind of testimony to avoid, and that is the testimony that denies God's grace.

Paul said, "But by the grace of God I am what I am, and His grace toward me was not in vain; but I labored more abundantly than they all, yet not I, but the grace of God which was with me" (1 Cor. 15:10). In other words, Paul said that though he was lacking in some significant attributes of leadership, God's grace was sufficient to enable him to lead.

As I said at some length in Chapter 9, I don't believe that Christians ought to respond to every compliment by saying, "It was only Jesus." But if the Christian isn't aware that we are what we are only by the grace of God, then he or she ought to remember that God's anger has often sent peacock feathers flying in the breeze.

Jill Briscoe once spoke at our church on the subject of humility. She said that when she gets compliments she thinks of them as flowers and simply says "Thank you" for the flower. All day she gathers those flowers, and at night she presents them to Jesus. I like that because it reflects the awareness that (as a friend of mine expresses it) if you see a turtle on a gatepost, you know he didn't get there by himself.

God's grace is the motivating element in Christian boldness. His grace creates the boldness. And because bold Christians risk a lot, they often fail, but His grace covers the failure too.

I have started writing with a word processor. I always said I would never use a computer, and here I am typing away in front of the computer screen. As I said earlier in this book, I am probably the least machine-oriented person you will ever know. In fact, my mother kept me away from wheelbarrows because she knew my problem with machinery. Furthermore, I sometimes feel guilty about writing with anything other than a quill pen. Nevertheless, I have found that the amount of time using a computer saves me is worth it all.

This morning a friend of mine was watching me use the computer. He said, "Steve, I could never do anything like that. Those things confuse me."

"Listen," I replied, "if I can use one of these things, an ape can use one. I get confused turning the knobs of the television set. It frightened me at first, but just remember me if you ever think you can't do it."

Our testimony ought to be like that. We need to say to folks, "Look, I'm as frightened as you are. I'm a sinner, too, but God has sometimes given me what it takes to stand up and growl at the world. If He can do that with me, He can do that with you. Just try it. You'll be surprised."

Of course you are human and weak. I am aware that we are at different places in the process. I know you are a sinner and that my experience may be different from yours. But I also know that God's grace has given us both a tremendous freedom to be what God called us to be.

One of my problems is that I'm always looking for heroes. (If you know any "dirt" on C. S. Lewis, please keep it to yourself. I need at least one.) I have noticed that God is always destroying all my heroes—except Jesus. I remember how shocked I was when John De-Brine in answer to a question told me that one of my heroes was jealous of Billy Graham. He looked at my shocked face and said, "Steve, did you really think that he was an outsider to the sinful race?"

God is teaching me that real heroes aren't heroes because they are strong, sinless, experienced, or because they have traveled a long way down the road of Christian maturity. Real heroes are folks like you and me who have decided that we are going to stand for Christ no matter what, and the devil can take the hindmost.

He called us to be bold Christians. "Nice" is not enough. Nice guys not only finish last, but "nice" is not the point at all. If you have to choose between being nice or being bold, be bold. It will be okay.

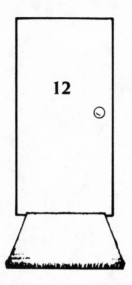

"O foolish Galatians! Who has bewitched you that you should not obey the truth, before whose eyes Jesus Christ was clearly portrayed among you as crucified? This only I want to learn from you: Did you receive the Spirit by the works of the law, or by the hearing of faith? Are you so foolish? Having begun in the Spirit, are you now being made perfect by the flesh?"

GALATIANS 3:1–3

Conformed to Their Image

12

When asked for a simple definition of the term *neurotic*, a famous psychiatrist once said, "A neurotic is a person who cannot say 'damn.'"[1] I probably ought not to say this, but I believe there is more truth in that than most Christians would think. There are certain taboos among Christians that reflect neurotic guilt. I am by no means suggesting that we ought to use "damn" more often. However, I am suggesting that whatever it is that makes Christians think that saying "damn" is a major aberration of God's law has become a bonanza for the manipulators of God's people—and that situation makes me angry.

You can find those taboos almost everywhere. For instance, what will happen if you don't have your devotions tomorrow morning? Is it possible, do you think, that you will get the fever and die? A friend of mine who has an office in downtown Dallas told me that one morning a friend of his entered his office and asked in a panic, "Do you have a Bible?" He allowed that he did, and his friend said, "Thank God. I forgot to read the Bible this morning, and I couldn't go to work without reading my Bible."

Let it not be said that I am against Bible reading. I advocate the practice from the pulpit and in my personal counseling. However, I do not advocate it because it is some kind of magic formula whereby God rears back and passes a "blessing miracle" on you because you read the Bible for the day. The daily Bible reading should be a time when you listen to the Father. If it becomes an act of magic to keep you from getting hurt during the day, there is a great danger that the manipulators are going to "clean your clock."

As I have mentioned before, our church has a ministry in the arts. We often will have concerts and plays in our sanctuary that could not be described as strictly Christian. For instance, some of the concerts are secular jazz concerts, and some of the plays are the same plays that one would find at your local center for the performing arts. Occasionally we will have creative dance in one of our worship services. We have not gone into this ministry without thinking and praying about it. We have simply come to the conclusion that the problem with most Americans is not that they don't think about Jesus. The problem is that they don't think about anything. Our arts program is an effort to get people to think with the hope that if they start thinking, maybe then we can get them to think specifically about Jesus.

I was teaching part of a leadership course in a Christian college when one of the students who was from our city asked some hostile questions during a question and answer period. I wasn't sure why he was angry at me until after the class. He came up to me and said, "Pastor Brown, the last time I was home on vacation I visited your church, and I don't think your church is biblical."

"I'm accused of a lot of things," I said, "but 'not being biblical' is usually not one of them. If you'll tell me where we've been unbiblical, I'll see that we change."

"When I was home I went to your church for a concert," he

said, his voice and demeanor becoming more and more intense as he talked. "I heard that there was a concert at the Key Biscayne Church. I was glad, because I was looking for something that would lift my spirits and turn my thoughts toward God. When I got there, I was horrified that it was not a Christian concert but a worldly concert. I just think that you have a responsibility to honor God in what you do. Jazz does not honor God. If I had wanted to listen to jazz, I would have gone to a bar."

"I'm sorry you were offended," I said, "but I think your offense is founded in your cultural likes and dislikes and not in the Bible. However, if you can show me where the Bible says that we shouldn't have jazz concerts, I will stop them."

His face went absolutely blank. Nobody had ever asked him specifically where the Bible confirmed his legalism. He stammered and stuttered trying to think of a verse that wasn't there.

I said to him, "Son, would you like me to tell you why jazz concerts are biblical?" He agreed that that would be good if I could do it: So I showed him where Jubal was the father of all those (both Christian and pagan) who play the harp and the flute (Gen. 4:21). I showed him how we are commanded to praise God with the "sound" of the trumpet, the stringed instruments, and the flutes (Ps. 150:3–4). I pointed out that David and all of Israel "played music before the LORD on all kinds of instruments made of fir wood, on harps, on stringed instruments, on tambourines, on sistrums, and on cymbals" (2 Sam. 6:5).

"Let me ask you a question," I said. "Would you tell me what is Christian about the musical note A?" He looked puzzled as I continued, "To be perfectly honest with you, there is nothing particularly Christian about the note A except that that note was created by God. When a Christian plays the note A and he or she does it well, whether that note is found in a hymn or a piece of jazz, it becomes a Christian's offering to God. And that is why we have jazz concerts in our church."

My young friend said that he would think about it. I'm glad, because Christians need to think. Legalism (i.e., that kind of Christianity that measures faithfulness by "dos" and "don'ts") is often a reflection of something quite different from what is taught in the Bible. Jay Kesler, the former president of Youth for Christ and now president of Taylor University, once said that if the Christian faith were determined by not doing anything wrong, the finest Christian in his household was his dog.

Glenda Sturtevant tells the story of a pastor who was greatly concerned about a new stereo system in one of the social rooms in his church. He was afraid that it would be broken or stolen, so he made a large sign and placed it near the stereo. It read, "This is the eleventh commandment: Thou shalt not touch the stereo system. Signed, The Pastor." A few weeks later, someone wrote on the bottom of the sign: "Thou shalt not make additional commandments. Signed, The Lord."[2]

If you have been a Christian for very long, you know it isn't easy. When one tries to live by what the Bible says, it is a monumental task. What makes it worse is that there are people who want to add to what the Bible says. They want to increase, as it were, the number of commandments. Jesus said, "Woe to you, scribes and Pharisees, hypocrites! For you pay tithe of mint and anise and cumin, and have neglected the weightier matters of the law: justice and mercy and faith" (Matt. 23:23).

Legalism is one of the great destroyers of boldness. You will find it in the Christian who is constantly asking if he or she is doing it right or wrong, and who becomes, like the centipede, crippled for want of knowing which foot to put forward. You will find legalism creeping into the life of the new Christian whose joy and freedom are destroyed because some "mature" Christian gave the impression that "real" Christians, in their obedience, have given up everything that was fun, fattening, or free. You will find the disease of legalism measuring sin by how much one enjoyed it. (That is, if it was enjoyed, it was a sin. If it was not enjoyed, it was not a sin or, certainly, not a bad one.) Legalism comes from the mouth of Satan, the accuser, who tells the Christian, "If you were really a Christian, you wouldn't act that way." You will find legalism in the pulpit and in the pew as Christians become desperately concerned with their and others' purity and rightness. The question of ultimate concern for the legalist is, "What will others say?" The great commandment for the legalist is, "Thou shalt be like me."

Legalism can kill the necessary freedom of boldness. Let's talk about it.

THE CHRISTIAN MAGNA CHARTA

The book of Galatians is an exciting book because it contains some of the most freeing teaching in all the Scripture. It has been called "the Magna Charta of Christian liberty." In that book Paul addressed the Galatians about one of the most priceless gifts of God, freedom.

Some thirteen years from the date of Paul's conversion, Barnabas came to get Paul and enlist his help with the believers in Antioch. God had deemed that it was time for Paul to be used in the service of the King. A lot happened at Antioch, but one of the major happenings was that the believers sent Paul and Barnabas on the first missionary journey of the church.

On that first missionary journey, Paul and Barnabas visited the towns in the southern part of Galatia, a Roman province. They established churches in Pisidia, Antioch, Iconium, Lystra, and Derbe.

After the completion of that first journey, Paul and Barnabas returned to Syrian Antioch and told how God had manifested His grace to the people of Galatia. Everyone was excited about what God was doing.

And then the disturbing reports started coming in. They told of how the new Christians in Galatia were turning away from the excitement and freedom of their first love. The reports told of the horror of "legalism" and how it was destroying the joy of the believers. Paul, with the love and firmness of a mother correcting her children, sat down and wrote a letter. The letter he wrote is in your Bible and is known as Galatians. It was probably the earliest letter of Paul that we have in the Bible, and, as such, it reflects the thoughts of Paul in their earliest and, in one sense, clearest form.

In my mind's eye, I can see the great apostle bending over a small writing table using the light of a flickering candle. I can see him pausing often in his writing to think—and sometimes to calm his anger. If you read the book of Galatians, it is possible to think of Paul as an angry, vindictive man. He wrote such things as "But even if we, or an angel from heaven, preach any other gospel to you than what we have preached to you, let him be accursed" (1:8–9). His imagery was not what one would want to be used in church. In referring to the circumcision he blurts out, "I could wish that those who trouble you would even cut themselves off!" (5:12).

The tone of Galatians is harsh, but it was the harshness that comes from a broken heart. Paul's heart was broken over the destruction taking place among God's people. If you had watched him write and you had looked closely, you would have seen tears falling on the parchment on which Paul penned his letter.

In what follows I want to take my cue from Paul's letter to the Galatians in both content and attitude. There is probably nothing in all of Christendom that "ticks me off" more than unthinking legalism. I believe it has hurt more Christians than we would ever believe. I don't want to be anything less than strong and clear in what I say about it.

On the other hand, I also realize that the disease of legalism is, more often than not, seen in Christians who love Christ the most. Recently, some people in a conference at which I was speaking had been very critical of some other Christians who were taking the gospel to the world in different cultural forms. They were using rock music to proclaim Christ. (Incidentally, you should know that many of the hymns we are now using in our churches were the beer-drinking tunes of the eighteenth century.)

That evening I had decided that I was going to get those "narrow-minded turkeys." But before I spoke, the Father spoke. He said, "Son, you must remember that these people who make you so angry are the people who love Me the most. They are My flock, and you must not beat them. I didn't call you to beat people, I called you to teach. Do what I told you to do." So let's consider some of the teaching in the book of Galatians.

BAD NEWS AND VERY BAD NEWS

Did you hear about the man who went to his doctor and the doctor told him that he had some bad news and some very bad news? The man asked to hear the bad news first, and the doctor said, "The bad news is that I have examined your tests and you have twenty-four hours to live."

"Man!" exclaimed the man, "That is really bad news. What in the world could be worse than that?"

"The very bad news is," said the doctor, "I should have talked to you yesterday."

As we talk about the book of Galatians, I have some bad news and some very bad news. But hang on. Before we finish, I also have some very good news for you.

The Bad News

The bad news concerns the law.

> For as many as are of the works of the law are under the curse; for it is written, "Cursed is everyone who does not continue in all things which are written in the book of the law, to do them." But that no one is justified by the law in the sight of God is evident, for "The just shall live by faith." Yet the law is not of faith, but "The man who does them shall live by them" (3:10–12). "What purpose then does the law serve? It was added because of transgressions" (3:19). "Is the law then against the promises of God? Certainly not! For if there had been a law given which could have given life, truly righteousness would have been by the law" (3:21). "Therefore the law was our tutor to bring us to Christ, that we might be justified by faith. But after faith has come, we are no longer under a tutor" (3:24–25).

The bad news is that we are under a curse, and the curse is the law. Paul said, "For as many as are of the works of the law are under the curse" (3:10). There is something in us that confirms our most horrible fears. There is a righteous and holy God, and His demands are righteous and holy. There is a sense in all of us that somehow we have offended Him, and that we will someday have to answer for it.

Silly, old fashioned nonsense.

Right? Wrong, and you know it in your heart.

In fact, I believe that legalism has as its root cause the knowledge that we have to be better than we are lest we offend a holy and righteous God. If going to church is not enough, then honoring the "Lord's day" ought to be added to going to church. If you still feel you don't have it, you decide that what one ought to do is to read the Bible and pray all day Sunday and give up television. And then you still don't feel holy, so you give up television all week and read the Bible and pray a few more hours. If that still doesn't cut it, you fast one day a week, and if that doesn't work you add movies, make-up, dancing, smoking, drinking, novels, card-playing, and "secular" music to the list of things you ought to give up. And then if you have done all of that and you still don't feel you please a holy and righteous God, you try to get others to go to church, read the Bible, and pray on Sunday, give up television on Sunday, give up television the rest of the week, pray more and read the Bible more, give up movies, make-up, dancing, smoking, drinking, novels, card playing, and "secular" music. If they refuse, of course, they have misused their liberty.

Paul called the process the "curse" of the law, and it is a real curse. It is the awareness of how much the real God demands and the imposed necessity of trying to meet those demands. That is the bad news.

Very Bad News

The very bad news is that you can't do it. It would be good if we could, because the law is not bad in the sense that what God tells us we ought and ought not to do will be harmful. In fact, just the opposite is true. If we could live by the law perfectly, we would be perfectly happy. God's law is the best way to live. The problem is that we are not good enough to live by it. Note what Paul said about the law: "But that no one is justified by the law in the sight of God is evident" (3:11). The law, whether it is the law of God as expressed in Holy Torah or the law expressed in devout Christians who have heaped laws upon laws to help us be faithful to *the* law, is a curse in the sense that it is a puzzle that can't be completed, a book that can't be read, a road that can't be traveled, a mountain that can't be climbed, and a task that can't be done.

A friend of mine once posed a riddle to me. He said, "What is yellow, has feathers, sings, plays baseball, and lives in a cage?" I thought for a long time. He said, "Give up?"

I said, "I can't imagine the answer to your riddle. I give up. What is it?"

"A canary."

"A canary?" I sputtered, "A canary doesn't play baseball!"

"Oh," he said laughing, "I lied about the baseball."

The law and the laws we make up to keep the law are like that. There are all kinds of promises. If you just work hard enough at it, if you add to your list of "don'ts" and subtract from your list of "dos," eventually you will be clean, pure, honest, sweet, kind, loving, obedient, and faithful. Then God will notice how good you are doing and how hard you are trying, and He will love you.

And then we try—we really try. At the end of our trying, we know we have failed. And the law says, "I lied about the success."

I have a friend who decided that he would not work or cause anyone else to work on the Lord's day. So he stopped taking the Sunday paper because he didn't want to cause the paperboy or the reporters to work on Sunday. He stopped taking the bus to church because he didn't want the bus driver to work on Sunday, and he quit going to restaurants on Sunday so he wouldn't make those folks work.

To help him see the futility of this approach, I asked if he used electricity in his house on Sunday. He agreed that he did, and I reminded him that he was causing the people at the power company to work on Sunday. I told him that a lot of the features used in the newspaper on Sunday were written during the week. Not only that, I said, but the Sunday paper is printed on Saturday, so if he really wanted to be consistent he would have to stop taking the Monday paper. In fact, he would have to stop taking the paper altogether, because by buying the paper he contributed to the institution that supported the reporters who wrote during the week for the Sunday paper and thereby caused others to work on Sunday. I suggested that he ought to give up the bus all the time. After all, the mechanics had to work on Sunday to make sure the bus would run on Monday. "The restaurants," I went on, "have to prepare a lot of their food on Saturday—"

"Wait a minute," he said, "I get your point. I give up."

My friend was beginning to see the very bad news. All of us have seen the very bad news whenever we have tried to live up to God's standard as given to us in the Bible, or to man's standard as given to us by the legalists. We want to cry out with Paul, "O wretched man that I am! Who will deliver me from this body of death?" (Rom. 7:24).

Dear friend, you can't live up to the standards. I know how hard you have been working at it. I know all you have given up—all the pain and hurt. I know the people who have called you a fanatic and the pagans who have made fun of you. I know the times when you have denied yourself, when you have turned away from worldliness. I know the tears you have shed and the times you have asked forgiveness and promised to be better, only to find yourself back in the same old trap. I know the number of times you have gone over the "check list" to make sure you didn't miss anything, and the horror you felt when you discovered that you had. I know the sleepless nights and the dull, unhappy days. I also know you did it for God. The very bad news is that all your efforts are for nothing. You have been reaching for a golden ring, and the golden ring is just an illusion.

THE GOOD NEWS

I promised to give you the bad news and the very bad news, and I have. But I also promised to give you the very good news. Paul called the law a curse, but he also suggested it is a blessed curse. "Is the law then against the promises of God? Certainly not! For if there had been a law given which could have given life, truly righteousness would have been by the law. . . . Therefore the law was our tutor to bring us to Christ" (Gal. 3:21, 24).

Author Frederick Buechner described how his mother and brother dealt with his father's suicide. They moved to Bermuda. His grandmother was a harsh and, in some ways, wise woman who had learned from her father that the best way to deal with the harshness of life was to stare it right in the eye and face it down. "She was right that reality can be harsh and that you shut your eyes to it only at your peril because if you do not face up to the enemy in all of his dark power, then the enemy will come up from behind some dark day and destroy you while you are facing the other way."[3]

Buechner's grandmother told the family to stay in New York and face reality. But Buechner pointed out something that runs through the very core of the universe. He wrote:

> To do for yourself the best that you have it in you to do—to grit your teeth and clench your fists in order to survive the world at its harshest and worst—is, by that very act, to be unable to let something be done for you and in you that is more wonderful still. The trouble with steeling yourself against the harshness of reality is that the same steel that secures your life against being destroyed secures your life also against being opened up and transformed by the holy power that life itself comes from.[4]

What Buechner said about standing against reality without giving in can be said about the way we deal with the law and the laws. When you can't do any more, you discover something wonderful. Jesus Christ has done it for you. Paul said, "Christ has redeemed us from the curse of the law, having become a curse for us" (Gal. 3:13).

199

NO MORE MR. NICE GUY!

C. S. Lewis had a great comment on those who try to live by the law. He said that one way or the other, one of two results will follow.

> Either we give up trying to be good, or else we become very unhappy indeed. For, make no mistake: If you are really going to try to meet all the demands made on the natural self, it will not have enough left over to live on. The more you obey your conscience, the more your conscience will demand of you. And your natural self, which is thus being starved and hampered and worried at every turn, will get angrier and angrier. In the end, you will either give up trying to be good, or else become one of those people who, as they say, "live for others" but always in a discontented, grumbling way—always making a martyr of yourself. And once you have become that you will be a far greater pest to anyone who has to live with you than you would have been if you had remained frankly selfish.[5]

So, what do you do? Let me tell you. Give everything you have to Christ. Accept His acceptance. Give up the battle and begin to live. He has promised to give you His Spirit. That is a reality you don't have to think about all the time any more than you have to think about how to ride a bicycle when you're on it. You simply ride the bicycle.

The Christian lives a life of faith. Faith in what? Faith in the promise of Christ that you are accepted not on the basis of how good you are, but on the basis of how good He was. Every once in a while you need to check the law of the Bible because it reflects God's will. When Jesus said that He had not come to destroy the law but to fulfill it, He meant that He had come to give His people the power to live by God's law (still the best way to live) and forgiveness when they didn't. The law (not the laws we create) is a good measurement. He wants you to check it *not so you can see how bad you are doing, but so you can see how well you are doing by His grace.*

The famous statement of Augustine's about loving God and doing as you please is true. When you love Him, that is all you have to do. In a response to His love, give Him yourself—everything. His love will hold you and mold you and change you. Paul put it this way, "I have been crucified with Christ; it is no longer I who live, but Christ lives in me; and the life which I now live in the flesh I live by faith in the Son of

God, who loved me and gave Himself for me" (Gal. 2:20). Now you can be free to be bold.

My friend Jim Green told me about an interesting incident that happened on the first live nationwide television broadcast. Because it was a first, a number of prominent people were asked to address the nation. Conrad Hilton was among those who had that opportunity. Everyone waited to see what this great man would say to such a tremendous audience. He said, "A number of you have stayed at Hilton hotels. Let me ask you to do something for me. When you take a shower, make sure the shower curtain is on the inside of the tub."

Can you believe that? What a great opportunity, and he talks about shower curtains! It reminds me of those folks who take the precious gift of freedom and joy given to the Christian and who make a mockery of it by destroying it with rules and regulations.

Do you know what God would have said given the same setting? He would have said, "A number of you have stayed at Hilton hotels. I'm glad, and I want you to enjoy it and have a good time. If you have a problem, just let me know about it."

Of course, the Christian life is not a Hilton hotel. It is a lot more serious than that. However, God does own the hotel, and He makes the rules. Just make sure that they are His rules you are following and not those of one of the bellboys. His rules are not all that tough. In fact there is only one. He wants you to die, so He can live through you. Once He begins to live through you, you own the hotel too.

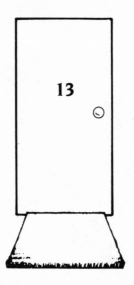

"Oh, the depth of the riches both of the wisdom and knowledge of God! How unsearchable are His judgments and His ways past finding out!"

ROMANS 11:33

God and the Gurus

13

Do you know what really irritates me? People who think they have God in their back pockets irritate me. It's not that they say dumb things. Everybody is entitled to say some dumb things. It isn't that they're arrogant and rude. I believe only God can judge hearts, and sometimes rudeness and arrogance are a reflection of a broken heart. It doesn't even bother me that they don't allow others to have opinions. I appreciate strong convictions. What really bothers me is that somehow they have been convincing to a lot of people. What bothers me is that so many people really believe that some people have God in their back pockets.

On one occasion early in my ministry, I got confused about the time of a funeral. I thought it was to be held in the afternoon but it was actually scheduled for the morning. I was sitting in my study half listening to someone who was talking to me when I glanced down at my calendar to find that at that very moment I was to be conducting a funeral. That was bad enough, but to make it worse, the funeral home was on the other side of town.

I grabbed my robe and Bible and headed for the door, yelling at my secretary that if the funeral director called, tell him I was on my way. It was a miracle I wasn't killed that day given the speed at which I drove across town. When I drove (no, *drove* isn't the word—*screeched* is better) into the parking lot of the funeral home, I noticed that the parking lot was full and the funeral director was standing there with his arms crossed. His comment was classic: "Reverend, be calm. Act like you were unavoidably detained. There are three people here today who can do no wrong: you, me, and the corpse."

Unfortunately there are people in the church who give the impression that there are only three people who can do no wrong: God, the one who has God in his or her back pocket, and the people who have canonized the teachings of the one who has God in his or her back pocket.

This belief that certain individuals have God in their back pockets is a disease in the church that has created "heresy hunters" who are not happy unless every "t" is crossed and every "i" is dotted. It is a disease that causes all of us to distrust the rest of us. That would be bad enough, but the disease has made all of us so careful about where we walk, what we say, how we look, and with whom we associate that we hardly have time for anything else. Boldness on the battlefield requires that soldiers fight the enemy. If you don't know if the enemy is in front of you or behind you, you have a tendency to be very careful. Careful is not enough in a world where there is a lusty, materialistic paganism with destruction on its mind.

Now, before we go any further, it is important that you understand what I am going to be saying in the pages of this chapter. Someone has said that before you criticize what I say, you should demonstrate that you have understood what I said. I think that is important. So, in an effort at understanding, I want to tell you what I'm *not* going to be saying in this chapter.

First, I am not going to be saying that I think the eternal verities of the Christian faith are up for grabs. I believe that the Bible is revealed, propositional truth. It is the canon by which all other truth is measured. Verbal, plenary inspiration of Scripture is, I believe, the teaching of the Bible and of historic Christianity. If you think that I have said something other than that, you haven't understood me.

Second, I believe that systematic biblical theology is not only important, but that it is even mandated by the necessities of presenting to the world a credible, rational statement of Christianity. Too many Christians like to sing, "Jesus loves me this I know . . . and it is all I want to know." My theological position is Reformed, and while I don't believe it is the only legitimate way to understand Christianity, I do believe it is the most balanced and credible. While I say that, I give you the freedom to hold your position with equal fervor as long as it is within the bounds of biblical Christianity. If anything I say in this chapter causes you to think that I do not believe biblical theology is necessary, you have misunderstood me.

Third, I believe in strong leadership. I am tired of committees and debate. Committees are often the methodology whereby individuals escape responsibility, and debate is the way we postpone having to do anything. While I do not believe in blind submission to any authority other than God's, I do believe in authority and its necessary operation for the health and wholeness of the church. If you think I have said something other than that, you have misunderstood me.

Finally, I believe that there are appropriate biblical ways of coping with the vicissitudes of life. I do not believe the Christian can operate outside the biblical standards in dealing with life. "Whatever works for you" and "whatever turns you on" is the pagan way of dealing with life. I believe in Christian liberty, and I am libertarian in many of my views—but I am not a libertine.

Those distinctions are important. If you feel, after reading what follows, that I am a libertine advocating unrestrained freedom, I have failed to communicate or you have misunderstood me.

GOD IN THEIR POCKETS?

I mentioned above three persons who can do no wrong: God, the Christian leader who believes he or she has God in his or her back pocket, and those who have canonized the teachings of those who believe they have God in their pockets. I also said the latter two are a real menace to Christian boldness. Let's talk about it.

The Sovereignty and Greatness of God

First, it is terribly important that Christians understand the greatness and the absolute sovereignty of God. I love Paul's doxology in Romans:

> Oh, the depth of the riches both of the wisdom and knowledge of God! How unsearchable are His judgments and His ways past finding out! "For who has known the mind of the LORD? Or who has become His counselor? Or who has first given to Him and it shall be repaid to Him?" For of Him and through Him and to Him are all things, to whom be glory forever. Amen (Rom. 11:33–36).

Some of the harshest judgments of the Bible are reserved for those who have worshiped someone other than God or who have accepted the worship due only to God. "I am the LORD your God, who brought you out of the land of Egypt, out of the house of bondage. You shall have no other gods before Me" (Exod. 20:2). "For you shall worship no other god, for the LORD, whose name is Jealous, is a jealous God" (Exod. 34:14). "For the LORD your God is a consuming fire, a jealous God" (Deut. 4:24).

In the book of Acts, Herod was in the process of making peace with Tyre and Sidon. They flattered him because he controlled the food. Luke wrote:

So on a set day Herod, arrayed in royal apparel, sat on his throne and gave an oration to them. And the people kept shouting, "The voice of a god and not of a man!" Then immediately an angel of the Lord struck him, because he did not give glory to God. And he was eaten by worms and died. But the word of God grew and multiplied (Acts 12:21–24).

The Bible says, " 'For My thoughts are not your thoughts, nor are your ways My ways,' says the LORD. 'For as the heavens are higher than the earth, so are My ways higher than your ways, and My thoughts than your thoughts'" (Isa. 55:8). If that is true, and it is, then every Christian should approach God very carefully and others, on behalf of God, very hesitantly.

I have a preacher friend who says that the problem with being a preacher as opposed to a biblical prophet is that the prophets spoke whenever God called them to cry out, "Thus saith the Lord." He laughs and says, "I have to speak every Sunday whether or not the Lord gave me anything to say."

God doesn't need anybody's help. God is God, and whatever He proposes to do, He will do. Hotlines to God don't exist because God doesn't allow them to exist.

The Foolishness of Presumption

And that brings me to those who believe or give the impression that they have God in their back pockets. The Scripture speaks to the issue: "Do not be wise in your own eyes" (Prov. 3:7). "Do you see a man wise in his own eyes? There is more hope for a fool than for him" (Prov. 26:12). God said to Edom:

Behold, I will make you small among the nations; you shall be greatly despised. The pride of your heart has deceived you, you who dwell in the clefts of the rock, whose habitation is high; you who say in your heart, "Who will bring me down to the ground?" Though you exalt yourself as high as the eagle, and though you set your nest among the stars, from there I will bring you down (Obad. 1:2–4).

Paul wrote, "And if anyone thinks that he knows anything, he knows nothing yet as he ought to know" (1 Cor. 8:2).

God's message to Jeremiah ought to make every man or woman who claims to speak for God very careful. Jeremiah 23:30–34 reads:

"Therefore behold, I am against the prophets," says the LORD, "who steal My words every one from his neighbor. Behold, I am against the prophets," says the LORD, "who use their tongues and say, 'He says.' Behold, I am against those who prophesy false dreams," says the LORD, "and tell them, and cause My people to err by their lies and by their recklessness. Yet I did not send them or command them; therefore they shall not profit this people at all," says the LORD.

"So when these people or the prophet or the priest ask you, saying, 'What is the oracle of the LORD?' you shall then say to them, 'What oracle?' I will even forsake you," says the LORD. And as for the prophet and the priest and the people who say, 'The oracle of the LORD!' I will even punish that man and his house."

Chuck Colson tells of a New York bishop who spoke for a gay rights demonstration.

[The bishop] announced unequivocally that "AIDS is not God's judgment on the homosexual community." The idea that God might punish for such "so-called sins," he explained to his appreciative audience—and the grinding national television cameras—comes from "primitive, barbaric passages of the Old Testament."

The next day produced a predictable response from conservative church leaders. Indeed God has spoken, they thundered with righteous fervor; AIDS is His judgment on homosexuals.[1]

Colson went on to make the point that both the bishop and the conservative Christians claimed to speak for God. The question is, which one is right? Colson wrote, "Who speaks for God? He does quite nicely for Himself. Through His holy and infallible Word—and the quiet obedience of His servants."[2]

That's a good thing to remember. Malcolm Muggeridge has said that if Jesus were going through the wilderness temptation today, Satan would have had four temptations, and the fourth would be the opportunity to appear on national television. What a great temptation. After all, it would give Him an opportunity to reach millions of people with one shot. He could have proclaimed His message in a way that would have eliminated the necessity of all that travel. And then there would be the money. Think of what He could have done with all the money in the service of bringing in the Kingdom.

I would not suggest that all media ministries are wrong. But as one who has a national radio ministry, I am aware of some great dangers. "Experts" get created overnight, and then when the letters come in telling you how wonderful you are, there is the tendency to believe them. At first you say, "Well, of course, they don't know me." Then you say, "But they may have a point." And finally you are sure that the people who think you are wonderful have great taste, and may God have mercy on anybody who dares question or criticize. After all, you do speak for God.

I'm sure that Jim Jones knew the truth about Jim Jones when he was starting his work. It begins with a genuine desire to serve God, and it ends with grape Kool-Aid.

It is very dangerous for any man or woman to stand between God and His people. That doesn't mean that God doesn't use men and women to speak His message, but that it is always in the context of accountability and confirmation within the Body of Christ. Just because a man or woman can get a crowd (Hitler got a crowd) doesn't mean that the man or woman speaks for God. Just because a Christian leader sounds spiritual (Satan sounds spiritual) doesn't mean that God has blessed the sound. Just because a pastor, teacher, or evangelist seems certain (Lee Harvey Oswald seemed certain) doesn't mean that he or she ought to be followed.

Edward Bratcher gives a wonderful prayer in his book *The Walk-on-water Syndrome*:

Oh Lord God, Thou hast made me a pastor and teacher in the church. Thou seest how unfit I am to administer rightly this great responsible office; and had I been without Thy aid and counsel I would surely have ruined it long ago. Therefore do I invoke Thee.

> How gladly do I desire to yield and consecrate my heart and mouth to this ministry. I desire to teach the congregation. I, too, desire ever to learn and to keep Thy Word my constant companion and to meditate thereupon earnestly.
> Use me as Thy instrument in Thy service. Only do not Thou forsake me, for if I am left to myself, I will certainly bring it all to destruction. Amen.[3]

Someone has said that we live in the era of celebrities as opposed to models and heroes. A model or a hero is someone who has accomplished something in a particular field and who, therefore, is worthy of emulation. A celebrity is a person who is known for being known. It can happen in the church too. Becoming known is a lot easier than it used to be. With the media (both Christian and secular) creating new celebrities every day, there are lots of people who are known for being known. Christians' seemingly insatiable need to create gurus often brings us to the frightening prospect that whoever speaks the last, the loudest, and is the best known is the expert.

I don't think there is necessarily anything wrong with being known for being known, unless people start believing that because someone is known they *know*. And that brings me to the third, and real danger: the danger of people's accepting somebody other than God as their guru.

Pitfalls for Followers

The Scripture has some very harsh things to say, not only about false leaders, but also about those who follow them. "O My people! Those who lead you cause you to err, and destroy the way of your paths. . . . [Therefore] your men shall fall by the sword, and your mighty in the war. Her [Zion's] gates shall lament and mourn, and she being desolate shall sit on the ground" (Isa. 3:12b;25–26). Again from Isaiah: "For the leaders of this people cause them to err, and those who are led by them are destroyed. Therefore the LORD will have no joy in their young men, nor have mercy on their fatherless and widows; for everyone is a hypocrite and an evildoer, And every mouth speaks folly. For all this His anger is not turned away, but His hand is stretched out still" (Isa. 9:16–17). In Jeremiah there is a sobering word from God: "An astonishing and horrible thing has been committed in the land: The prophets prophesy falsely, and the priests rule by their own power; *and My people love to have it so*" (Jer. 5:30–31, italics mine).

I have some problems with Mary McDermott Shideler's very honest book *In Search of the Spirit*, but her testimony about her search is helpful. She said that unless we learn "that if we capitulate to a word that does not reverberate in our own hearts, we diminish ourselves as persons." In referring to her own search for the reality of God, she wrote:

> When, however, I made the critical error of surrendering myself wholly to an authority of whatever kind—parent, spouse, political or social leader, psychological or religious arbiter—I learned much about those others' flaws and faults but little about my own. And by participating in the world primarily through that authority, I denied myself full personal participation and so, without ceasing to participate, corrupted my identity and jeopardized my integrity. Had I taken those authorities only as guides or mentors, I could have retained my identity and integrity, and benefited exceedingly from their admonitions. My mistake was in giving them an absolute authority.[4]

LESSONS LEARNED

I have gone down a lot of wrong roads following a lot of sincere but mistaken people. Let me tell you some things I have found to be helpful. First, there are no infallible teachers or leaders. God had only one perfect preacher. His name was Jesus. People were drawn to Him because "He taught them as one having authority, and not as the scribes" (Matt. 7:29). Be careful about everybody else.

Second, false teachers and leaders are not to be judged on the basis of the size of the crowd, the bigness of the church, the glibness of the tongue, the sincerity of the voice, the certainty of the demeanor, or the glitter of the ministry. God's people are to be fruit inspectors. Jesus said:

> Beware of false prophets, who come to you in sheep's clothing, but inwardly they are ravenous wolves. You will know them by their fruits. Do men gather grapes from thornbushes or figs from thistles? Even so, every good

tree bears good fruit, but a bad tree bears bad fruit. A good tree cannot bear bad fruit, nor can a bad tree bear good fruit (Matt. 7:15–18).

Do you see biblical love and humility? Is financial integrity an important ingredient? Are the sheep being fed or fleeced? Is there a "messiah complex" extant in the ministry? Is there accountability? Are the followers automatons or free, thinking individuals?

Third, when authority (other than God's authority) is asked to be accepted without explanation, that authority is usually not from God. Watchman Nee said that one of the ways to tell whether a message came from God or from Satan was to remember that Satan says, "Do it now!" and God says, "Think about it, and then do it." That is good advice for guidance from God or from man. "Because I say so" may be good for children and mindless animals, but not for God's people. Legitimate spiritual authority is always willing to be questioned. Legitimate spiritual authority never asks from you what you should only give to God.

Finally, learn what the Scripture says. Don't just learn it from a Bible teacher, a commentary, or a religious book (including this one). Go to the Bible yourself and find out what God says. You will be surprised more than you think by how often a spiritual leader will pontificate something that makes God blush. God gave you a mind, and more important than that, He gave you His Spirit. Paul said that the Christian has received the Spirit of Christ and therefore ought to be able to perceive truth, "For 'Who has known the mind of the LORD that he may instruct Him?' But we have the mind of Christ" (1 Cor. 2:16).

I am not against good Christian books, of course (especially this one). One of the great gifts God has given His people is that of faithful Bible teachers. If you are really interested in God's Word, you ought to have some good commentaries in your library. However, and it is a big however, it is terribly important that you study the Bible for yourself and that you use the "mind of Christ" that is yours. Don't let someone else do your thinking for you.

A lot of people gave their lives so that we might have Bible translations in the common languages of the world. Luther's German translation of the Scripture, Lefèvre's French Bible, and Tyndale's English translation revolutionized the Christian church. Because of their work, Christians of their day were enabled to see the truth of God for the first time. Those Christians "checked it out" for themselves, and as a result the church will never be the same—unless, of course, we ignore their foundational work and revert to those days when Christians relied only on the "experts." The experts messed it up before. They still can.

THE DANGERS OF REVERING HUMAN TEACHING

Now let me say a word about some of the implications that flow from canonizing the teachings of those who believe they have God in their back pockets.

Institutionalism

First, there is the danger of institutionalism. Institutionalism is the hardening of the arteries of an institution. Christian institutions (churches, missions, seminaries, Christian schools, ministries) are certainly necessary to the proper functioning of what God is doing in the world. (Anytime three people get together to throw rocks at an institution, they have formed another institution.) The danger is that virtually all institutions tend to start showing the signs of institutionalism sooner or later.

Suppose I should have an encounter with God so real and so dynamic that I was able to bring others together under my leadership. Suppose further that I was able to lead other people into the same experience with God. Soon we would have a full-fledged institution going. (We could call it "The Sons and Daughters of Heavenly Hope.") Everything would probably be fine until my children and the children of my followers were old enough to enter the church. Assuming that these young people wanted to enter the church we had formed, they would not necessarily have had the same experience as ours. However, they would see we observed certain rituals, we said prayers in a certain way, we sang certain hymns, and we said certain things. It would be only natural that some of these young people should equate all of the ways we did things with the experience we had with God. By the time our grandchildren were old enough to enter the church, the ritual, the prayers, the hymns, and the words would have importance in and of themselves completely apart from any experience with God that we, the original founders of the church, had known.

Someone has said that the cycle of God's work begins with a man, followed by an institution, followed by a monument, followed by the necessity of God's finding another man. Well, maybe that is true, and even if it isn't always true, God's people still must be constantly aware of its danger.

The Superstition of Systems

Second, there is the danger of the superstition of systems. I am a Bible teacher, and any teacher will tell you that one of the best ways to teach anything of any importance is systematically. If you've read this far in the book, you're aware that I am fond of lists. You'll see lots of "first," "second," and "third". The danger in a system is that people have a tendency to forget that the system is one step (perhaps even more) removed from the original source. When one is teaching about God, the danger is multiplied.

God isn't a system. He is a person. That sounds like a truism, and it is. However, it is easy to forget. I have a friend who is truly, truly Reformed. (For the uninitiated, in Reformed circles we have the Reformed, the Truly Reformed, and the Truly, Truly Reformed. The Truly, Truly Reformed don't like or trust the Truly Reformed; the Truly Reformed don't like or trust the Reformed; and the Reformed don't like anybody else.) He told me once that it was impossible (he was talking about the doctrine of God's love for His people) for God to love the nonelect. God must have smiled and said, "You've got to be kidding!"

Lest those of you who are not Reformed feel too smug, let me suggest that you not throw rocks from your glass houses. Recently I heard a prominent television evangelist (who I wish would read just one theology book or church history book) say that my theological position is a heresy. I have been ruled out of the kingdom so many times because I didn't share a particular eschatological view or because my denomination was not the right one that I have lost count. Every week another dispensational or Arminian church divides with another dispensational or Arminian church because somebody suggested that Billy Graham or Jerry Falwell or Bob Mumford or Tony Campolo was not a man of God.

And if one more Charismatic tells me that I am a second class Christian because I am not "Spirit filled," I think I will die. And, of course, there is the system that says that any Charismatic experience must be either of the devil or the flesh. Then you throw Bill Gothard into the pot with his system and you have an interesting mix. And then somebody starts talking about "secondary separation." That means that you not only rule me out of the kingdom because I'm out of the kingdom, but you also rule me out of the kingdom if I know anybody who is already ruled out of the kingdom.

Paul said:

> But why do you judge your brother? Or why do you show contempt for your brother? For we shall all stand before the judgment seat of Christ. For it is written: "As I live, says the LORD, every knee shall bow to Me, and every tongue shall confess to God." So then each of us shall give account of himself to God. . . . Therefore let us pursue the things which make for peace and the things by which one may edify another (Rom. 14:10–12,19).

But the problem with systems goes further than basic theology or outlook. Everybody has a system that he or she teaches so that I can know the will of God, get wealthy, be successful, be healed, have a happy family, have good biblical sex, have a bigger church, discipline my child properly, and so on. (My friend Fred Smith says he is going to give a talk on ten ways to develop spontaneity.) The problem with the systems is that while they all claim to be biblical, they are at least that one step removed from the source.

What if there are six steps to knowing the will of God and the third and fourth don't work for me? What if the first five of the ten commandments for a happy marriage make mine worse? What if I follow Dr. Brown's Biblical System for the Discipline of One's Children and my children become Buddhists? Then I might have to fall back on God. That could be dangerous, because He might fail me. And to be perfectly honest with you, He isn't big on systems, and that makes me uncomfortable.

The Canonization of Extrabiblical Views

Finally, when one canonizes the teaching of someone who thinks that God is safely tucked away in his back pocket, there is the danger of canonizing other things that don't have anything to do with the guru's view of the Bible. For instance, it might be possible that someone could be a Christian without being a capitalist. God might not be a Democrat. There may be one Christian on an island somewhere who doesn't think dancing is a sin or that everybody who doesn't think that the biblical wine was grape juice is a heretic.

The point is that lifestyle, politics, and economics (along with a host of other items) are not the criteria by which one measures Christianity. There are, I believe, certain lifestyles and political and economic views that are more consistent with biblical teaching than others, and the Bible does draw clear standards to which the Christian must adhere. However, beyond those clearly taught standards, there is a lot more freedom than many of us believe.

I serve a church that is very orthodox about adherence to the Bible and its teaching. We practice church discipline and expect Christians to maintain a consistent, biblical style of life. We are very careful, however, to keep what is cultural Christianity separate from biblical Christianity. But after that requirement, there is a lot of freedom. Someone said of us recently, "They are different. They are very hard to define."

Thank God! It ought to be hard for pagans to define Christians except by commitment and faithfulness to Christ and our love for one another. When the definition gets much more specific than that, there is a blandness that the creator God who made penguins, giraffes, and you and me never intended.

Jesus said, "If the Son makes you free, you shall be free indeed" (John 8:36). He is your only Guru.

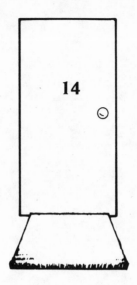

"I will preserve You and give You as a covenant to the people. . . . That You may say to the prisoners, 'Go forth,' to those who are in darkness, 'Show yourselves.'"

ISAIAH 49:8b–9a

A Declaration of Independence

14

One time Corrie ten Boom told me, after I had expressed shock about something she'd said, "Stephen, when you are an old lady, you can say anything." I suspected that she had not waited until she was an old lady before she expressed clearly and strongly whatever she felt God wanted her to say. It was just easier as she got older.

You don't have to wait either. And that is what this book has been about. If you have read this far, let me compliment you. Given the fact that I have someplace in these pages offended almost everyone, you are either a Tahitian worshiper of the Greek goddess Athena or you are the kind of Christian who is tired of being forced into anybody's mold except God's.

In Martin Bell's delightful book, *The Way of The Wolf*, he presents biblical truths in images that create fresh ways to think of Christ. In one of the chapters there is the story of a little boy who traveled with a wolf out of the warmth and safety of the forest. The story whispers of the incarnation: The silver wolf is God; the little boy who loses his magic, Jesus; and the wind, the

Holy Spirit. The story concerns the boy who lost the silver wolf (his magic), got murdered, and then got the magic back. Bell wrote:

> The boy stood quietly with his arms relaxed. There, barely discernible on a path leading out of the forest, was the silver wolf. Neither of them moved.
> "How much longer can we wait?" asked the boy.
> The wolf did not answer. He seemed to be sensing after something in the air. His powerful body was absolutely motionless.
> "I'm not at all sure that I like this," the boy went on, "Everything is so—well, so different! Even you don't know what it's going to be like there. Or what is going to happen to us. Maybe we shouldn't go. Have you ever thought about that? About not going, I mean?"
> The wolf was silent.
> "How much longer can we wait?" asked the boy. There was no reply.
> Then suddenly, wind. The silver wolf's fur stood on end. The boy shielded his eyes. Dead leaves swirled and scattered about his feet. The trees themselves seemed to be leaning over to touch him.
> Now apparently the wolf was satisfied. He still didn't speak. Nor did he change his expression. But his muscles went slack and he turned completely around. For one desperate moment the boy thought of running away. But that moment ended, and then the three of them were headed down the path that led out of the forest. The silver wolf. The wind. And the boy who was soon to lose his magic.[1]

Christians who have decided to be bold Christians are a lot like the little boy who was about to lose his magic. We too stand on the edge of our warm forest home and know that the silver wolf is going to lead us into dangerous, unknown, and frightening places. Of course, we are not going to lose our magic. We never had any. But it is, nevertheless, frightening.

But there is more than the fear. There is the realization that we were created in the image of God, and. . .

. . . whenever we become less than what He meant us to be,

. . . whenever we allow ourselves to be manipulated,

. . . whenever we engage in mindless submission either to the world or to other Christians,

. . . whenever we universalize someone else's experience and try to make it our own,

. . . whenever we refuse to laugh or to speak or to weep because we are afraid of what "they" will say,

. . . whenever we allow guilt or fear or worry to be the primary motivating factors in our lives,

. . . whenever we define humility, love, or servanthood in a way other than God's way,

. . . whenever we quit thinking and feeling,

. . . whenever we allow ourselves to be bound up in tradition,

. . . whenever we bow to any other God than the One who created us . . .

we have somehow betrayed that image.

When people accept Christ, we often tell them to do something to confirm that decision. We ask them to come forward and publicly profess their faith in Christ. Almost all of us, if we are believers, have done that. It was good because Jesus said, "Therefore whoever confesses Me before men, him I will also confess before My Father who is in heaven. But whoever denies Me before men, him I will also deny before My Father who is in heaven" (Matt. 10:32–33).

Most of us need to do it again. We shouldn't do it again for salvation. That is settled. But the world and the world's ways eat away at us, and after a while we have so conformed to somebody else's standards that we no longer see clearly. God has called us to be warriors. We are engaged in a battle. But as the years pass, we have so often taken the easy way that we don't have any war stories anymore.

Twila Paris has written a wonderful song titled, "The Warrior Is a Child":

> Lately I've been winning battles left and right.
> But even winners can get wounded in the fight.
> People say that I'm amazing,
> Strong beyond my years,
> But they don't see inside of me,
> I'm hiding all the tears.
>
> They don't know that I go running home when I fall
>   down.

They don't know Who picks me up when no one is
    around;
I drop my sword and cry for just awhile,
Cause deep inside this armor,
    The warrior is a child.[2]

Of course the warrior is a child. But when the child goes before the God of the universe, something special happens. He puts the magic in the fight. And the child once again becomes the warrior.

May I suggest a prayer:

Father, I confess before You that I have taken the heritage of freedom and boldness You gave me and have sold that heritage for a "mess of pottage." I have put others in the place reserved only for You. I have allowed people, even some of Your people, to mold me as they saw fit. I have allowed my precious freedom, the freedom Your Son bought with so great a price, to dissipate from neglect. I have remained silent when I should have spoken and, so often when I have spoken, I have spoken only to please others.

Father, I confess that I have acted out of fear when I knew that You would have given me courage if I had only asked.

I have acted out of guilt when I knew that You had forgiven me.

I have acted out of self-interest when I knew that I belonged to You.

I have put on the face of humility when I knew that I was only engaging in another kind of pride.

I have too often loved You with my heart without loving You with the mind that You gave me.

Father, I confess that I am afraid. Have mercy on me and forgive me for Christ's sake, and then, by Your grace, make me totally dependent on You and thereby independent of all that is not of You.

And, Father, when I get home, I promise to give You all the credit. I thank You for the strong, powerful name of Jesus in which I make this prayer. Amen.

That is, of course, a frightening prayer to pray. It is frightening because we know how weak and discouraged we are. However, He is never weak and discouraged, and it is to Him that we must go as a child that we might go to the world as His man or woman.

After you have prayed that prayer or one like it, let me suggest that you write a declaration—a declaration of independence—and put it in a place where you and others can see it. Maybe it would read something like this:

When, in the course of my life, it becomes necessary for me to dissolve the bonds that have bound me to people and things other than God, and to assume, among the powers of the earth, the separate and equal station to which the laws of nature and of nature's God entitle me, a decent respect to the opinions of mankind requires that I should declare the causes that have impelled me to the separation.

I hold these truths to be self-evident, that I was created equal to all other men and women and I have been endowed by my Creator with certain unalienable rights. Among these rights are my right to be different, to stand for my convictions, to bow my head before none other than God, and to be Christ's faithful disciple to my life's end.

Others have felt that they should stand between me and the God who created me.

Others have told me what only God can tell me.

Others have created systems that bind me to the rules and regulations of men.

Others have tried to make me feel guilty.

Others have threatened me with their rejection. They have told me that they would withhold their love from me if I was not like them.

Others have manipulated me and have made a mockery of God's special creation in me, and have thereby prevented me from acting freely and boldly in Christ's name.

I, therefore, a representative of the King, appealing to Him, do, in His name and by His authority, declare that I am free and independent of all except Him and those to whom He has bound me. To this declaration, with a firm reliance on the protection of Divine Providence, I do pledge my life, my fortune, and my sacred honor.

Now go out in the name of Christ and stand. When the war is over, we will gather around the throne and share the war stories. It would be horrible, then, only to listen to others' stories.

Notes

Chapter One

1. David R. Mains, *The Rise of the Religion of Antichristism* (Grand Rapids, Mich.: Zondervan Books, 1985), p. 17.
2. Aram Bakshian, Jr., "Gone with the Wimp," *National Review,* September 20, 1985, p. 50.
3. C. S. Lewis, *Perelandra* (New York: The Macmillan Company, 1965), p. 148.

Chapter Two

1. "Augustine" in *Great Books of the Western World,* ed. Robert Maynard Hutchins (Chicago: Encyclopaedia Britannica, Inc., 1952), 18, p. 130.
2. Fant and Pinson, *Twenty Centuries of Great Preaching* (Waco, Tex.: Word Books, 1971), I, 145.
3. C. S. Lewis, *The Best of C. S. Lewis* (New York: Christianity Today, Inc., 1969), pp. 184–5.

Chapter Three

1. William Kirk Kilpatrick, *Psychological Seduction* (Nashville, Tenn.: Thomas Nelson, 1985), p. 97.
2. Jones, Leisy, and Ludwig, eds., *Major American Writers* (New York: Harcourt, Brace and Co., 1952), p. 1256.
3. John Foxe, *Foxe's Christian Martyrs of the World* (Chicago: Moody Press, n.d.), p. 502.
4. Fant and Pinson, *Twenty Centuries of Great Preaching* (Waco, Tex.: Word Books, 1971), II, p. 193.
5. Quoted in James McGraw's *Great Evangelical Preachers of Yesterday* (Nashville, Tenn.: Abingdon Press, 1961), p. 40.

Chapter Four

1. Quoted anonymously in the newsletter of the National Foundation for the Study of Religion and Economics, September/October 1985.

2. Howard and Nisbet, eds., *On Freedom* (Greenwich, Conn.: Devin-Adair, 1984), p. 105.

3. Benedicta Ward, trans., *The Desert Christian: The Sayings of the Desert Fathers* (New York: Macmillan Publishing Co., 1975), p. 230.

4. C. S. Lewis, *The Weight of Glory* (Grand Rapids, Mich.: William B. Eerdmans Pub. Co., 1949), pp. 58, 63.

Chapter Five

1. Thomas R. Kelly, *A Testament of Devotion* (New York: Harper and Row, 1941), pp. 108–9.

2. Calvin Miller, *The Singer* (Downers Grove, Ill.: InterVarsity Press, 1978), pp. 75–7.

3. Kelly, pp. 64–5.

4. Philip Yancey, *Open Windows* (Nashville, Tenn.: Thomas Nelson Pub., 1985), p. 14.

Chapter Six

1. Hinsie and Campbell, eds., *Psychiatric Dictionary* (London: Oxford Univ. Press, 1970), 4th ed., p. 329.

2. Paul Tournier, *Guilt and Grace* (New York: Harper and Row, 1962), p. 70.

Chapter Seven

1. Franky Schaeffer, ed., *Is Capitalism Christian?* (Westchester, Ill.: Crossway Books, 1985), pp. 115–6.

2. Quoted in Douglas Archibald's *Yeats* (Syracuse, N.Y.: Syracuse Univ. Press, 1983), p. 75.

Chapter Eight

1. Jean Shepherd, "The Decline and Fall of the Wimp," *The Readers Digest*, Dec., 1985, (condensed from *The Newsday Magazine*), p. 120.

2. Bill Bryson, *The Book of Blunders* (New York: Dell Publishing Co., 1982), pp. 58–9.

3. Paul Brand and Philip Yancey, *In His Image* (Grand Rapids, Mich.: Zondervan Pub. House, 1984), p. 127.

Chapter Nine

1. R. C. Sproul, *In Search of Dignity* (Ventura, Calif.: Regal Books, 1983), p. 29.

2. Francois Fénelon, *Christian Perfection* (Minneapolis, Minn.: Dimension Books, 1975), p. 206.

3. A. W. Tozer, *A Treasury of A. W. Tozer* (Grand Rapids, Mich.: Baker Book House, 1980), p. 108.

4. John White, *The Masks of Melancholy* (Downers Grove, Ill.: InterVarsity Press, 1982), p. 113.

5. Tom Skinner, *Black and Free* (Grand Rapids, Mich.: Zondervan Pub. House, 1968), pp. 149, 151.

Chapter Eleven

1. C. H. Spurgeon, *Lectures to My Students* (London: Marshall, Morgan and Scott, 1969), p. 155.

Chapter Twelve

1. Quoted in Tournier's *Guilt and Grace*, p. 70.
2. Anderson and Wilcox, eds., *A Funny Thing Happened on the Way to Church* (St.Louis, Mo.: Concordia Pub. House, 1981), p. 54.
3. Frederick Buechner, *The Sacred Journey* (San Francisco: Harper and Row, 1952), p. 167.
4. Ibid., p. 46.
5. C. S. Lewis, *Mere Christianity* (New York: Macmillan Pub. Co., 1952), p. 167.

Chapter Thirteen

1. Charles Colson, *Who Speaks for God?* (Westchester, Ill.: Crossway Books, 1985), p. 20.
2. Ibid., p. 22.
3. Edward B. Bratcher, *The Walk-on-water Syndrome* (Waco, Tex.: Word Books, 1984), p. 64.
4. Mary McDermott Shideler, *In Search of the Spirit* (New York: Ballantine Books, 1985), pp. 29–30.

Chapter Fourteen

1. Martin Bell, *The Way of the Wolf* (New York: Ballantine Books, 1970), pp. 67–8.
2. Words and music by Twila Paris, © 1984, Singspiration.

Author

Stephen Brown, senior pastor of the Key Biscayne Presbyterian Church in Florida, is a popular speaker at churches, colleges, and conferences of various kinds across the country. Known for his ability to make the truths of Christianity extremely practical, he is also the speaker on a nationwide, daily, 15-minute radio program, "Key Life," and a visiting lecturer at Reformed Seminary and Denver Conservative Baptist Seminary.

Brown is a former radio disk jockey and news writer. He holds a Bachelor of Sacred Theology degree from the Boston University School of Theology. Married and the father of two daughters, he lives with his family in Coral Gables, Florida.

If you have enjoyed this book and would like to receive cassette tapes of Stephen Brown's sermons free of charge, send your name and address to Key Life Tapes, 160 Harbor Drive, Key Biscayne, Fla. 33149.